THE FUNDAMENTAL TRUTHS OF THE CHRISTIAN RELIGION

Sixteen Lectures delivered in the University of Berlin during the Winter Term 1901-2

BY

Dr. REINHOLD SEEBERG
PROFESSOR OF THEOLOGY IN THE UNIVERSITY OF BERLIN

Translated from the 4th Revised German Edition
BY
Rev. GEORGE E. THOMSON, B.D.
AND
CLARA WALLENTIN

Edited, with an Introductory Note
BY
Rev. W. D. MORRISON, LL.D.
RECTOR OF MARYLEBONE

WIPF & STOCK · Eugene, Oregon

Wipf and Stock Publishers
199 W 8th Ave, Suite 3
Eugene, OR 97401

The Fundamental Truths of the Christian Religion
Sixteen Lectures Delivered in the University of
Berlin During Winter Term 1901-2
By Seeberg, Reinhold and Thomson, George E.
ISBN 13: 978-1-60608-675-9
Publication date 3/2/2016
Previously published by Williams & Norgate, 1908

PREFACE TO THE ENGLISH EDITION

THE present volume consists of a series of sixteen lectures which I delivered in the University of Berlin, before students of all Faculties. From the fourth German edition the work has been translated into English by a former hearer of mine, Rev. George E. Thomson, Aberdeen. In its new dress and among new people, I wish the book as attentive readers as it has found in Germany, for the task it sets itself is certainly worthy of the reflection of all. Everywhere in our day we are confronted by the great task of preserving Christianity to the modern mind. This can be accomplished only if the modern world can be brought to the consciousness that even at the present day the deepest wants, needs, and problems which move man find their answer in the Gospel, and that the Gospel need fear no progress of science and culture. But for this purpose no pains must be spared in translating the thoughts of the Christian revelation into the speech and modes of thought of our own time. No element of real Christianity may thereby be surrendered, yet the particular way of stating the problem raised by the spirit and need of our time must receive minute attention. The old truth is to be taught in new wise.

Such an attempt is made in the present book. It is not addressed to any particular Church party, but is meant to stir up educated readers in all sections of the Church to examine their faith, and to show them that precisely in modern life they may again rejoice in it. The task which the book sets itself is thus, on the one hand, a religious, on the other hand a theological one. Theologically educated readers will easily discover in the book the framework of a new dogmatic system, and will be in a position to interpret and supplement the thoughts—however lightly they are often touched upon—in accordance with the system as a whole. The thought of a new "modern positive theology," as it has been present to my mind for years (*cf.* my *Kirche Deutschlands im 19ten Jahrhundert*, 2 ed., 1904, p. 302 ff.), has been, at least in its fundamental ideas, sketched in the present book. Theologians who wish to obtain more precise information about this question and the varied discussions which have been raised through it in German Theology, I refer to the thorough and luminous work of Prof. Beth in Vienna, *Die Moderne und die Principien der Theologie* (Berlin).

So may this little volume go forth and bear witness to English Christendom of the truth and power of our religion.

R. SEEBERG.

BERLIN, 18*th* May 1908.

INTRODUCTORY NOTE

As this is the first volume of Professor Seeberg's which has been translated into English, and as his name is not yet familiar to the English-speaking public, I have deemed it advisable in editing this little work to append a few preliminary words respecting the author of it. Dr Seeberg was born little less than half a century ago, and is therefore still in the maturity of his powers. After completing his preliminary education at Reval he commenced the study of theology, first at Dorpat and afterwards at Erlangen. In 1889 he became a professor of theology at Erlangen, and nine years afterwards he was called to occupy a chair of systematic theology at the University of Berlin. He has done a great deal of literary work, much of it contributed to reviews and encyclopædias. His principal publications are:—*A History of Christian Doctrine*; *A History of the German Church in the Nineteenth Century*; *The Holy Communion in the New Testament*; "A Sketch of Protestant Ethics" in the *Kultur der Gegenwart*; *Die Theologie des Duns Scotus*; *An Introduction to the History of Dogma*; and the volume which is now placed before the English public.

Professor Seeberg is rightly regarded among his own countrymen as one of the most thoughtful of contemporary theologians, and he exercises a wide influence on the modern German church. It will be seen from the present volume that he is more conservative in temper than some of the contemporary German theologians whose works have appeared in such a series as the Theological Translation Library. But he approaches the burning questions of religion and theology in a modern frame of mind. It is for this reason that his volume on *The Fundamental Truths of the Christian Religion* has gone through so many editions in Germany; and it is to be hoped that it will be equally successful in its English dress.

Hitherto, Dr Seeberg's publications have been mostly of an historical character; but his exhaustive and penetrating studies in historical theology have all been written with the object of shedding light upon the religious problems of the present. His studies of ecclesiastical dogma have led him to the conclusion that dogma is only the form in which the Christian society expresses its knowledge of the saving truths of faith. But these truths are quite capable of being separated from the historic forms in which they have found expression in the past. The theologians who have exercised the greatest influence on Professor Seeberg are Schleiermacher, Baur, and Hofmann; he is also in sympathy with Ritschl, but is out of touch with the developments of Ritschlianism as it is exhibited in the Ritschlian school. He blames them for an anti-metaphysical agnosticism and historicism; he considers their history too modern and their thought not modern enough. He objects to the Ritschlian principle of isolating theology from the other sciences, especially from metaphysics. Theology must be presented in the form of a general conception of the world; it is therefore impossible for it to attempt to dispense with metaphysics. On the other hand, he is at one with Ritschl and his followers in emphasising the practical character of the Christian religion. Religion, in Dr Seeberg's view, is the will of God ruling and directing the will of man; or, regarded from the human standpoint, it is the will of man attempting in the spirit of faith and love to realise the supreme purposes of God. But when the essentially practical character of religion has to be presented theoretically as a doctrinal system—and, in Dr Seeberg's opinion, it must, even for practical purposes, be embodied in a doctrinal system—a metaphysical background to this doctrinal system becomes a matter of necessity.

W. D. M.

CONTENTS

I

THE TRUTH OF THE CHRISTIAN RELIGION

LECTURE	PAGE
1. ORIGIN AND NATURE OF RELIGION	1
2. THE RELIGIONS OF MANKIND AND THE ABSOLUTE RELIGION	17
3. CHRISTIANITY AS THE ABSOLUTE RELIGION	34
4. THE PROOF OF THE ABSOLUTE RELIGION	55
5. FAITH AND LOVE	73
6. CHRISTIANITY AS POSITIVE RELIGION	94
7. CHURCH DOGMA	115

II

THE TRUTHS OF THE CHRISTIAN RELIGION

8. THE REVELATION OF GOD IN JESUS CHRIST	135
9. MAN FREE AND GOD ALL-OPERATIVE	154
10. THE NATURE OF HUMAN SIN	173

LECTURE	PAGE
11. Origin and Spread of Sin; The Redeemer of Sinners	192
12. The Person of Jesus Christ	211
13. The Work of Christ	237
14. The Church of Jesus Christ	264
15. The Origin and Development of the New Life of the Christian	289
16. The Moral Struggle for the New Life and its Goal	307

I

THE TRUTH OF
THE CHRISTIAN RELIGION

ORIGIN AND NATURE OF RELIGION 7

by any authorities, but exhibits a system of historical hypotheses. But to wander with the seven-league boots of possibility through the ocean of the possible, affords but uncertain prospect of landing on the shore of reality. There are many objections to this representation, though as yet the attempts to clear it out of the way have been unsuccessful. The history of religion in no way affords us only phenomena which witness to a straight line of progress, but marks of retrogression as well. Fetishism and spirit-worship, magic and superstition, are not wanting even at the height of development, but they show that a further development is not possible. Likewise it is difficult, according to this theory, to comprehend how present-day races that can look back over a long period of existence can do homage to this Fetishism, if it came at the very beginning. Have these races experienced no evolution at all? This would not agree with what missionaries tell us of the presence of higher ideas among them, which witness to the belief in an all-powerful Deity. One has but to think, for example, of the "Great Spirit" of the Indians; and similar and clearer ideas occur among quite crude negro races. They are called fossils, and that may be right; but fossils are witnesses to a once organic life. And finally, even here it is not at all clear how out of these spirits striving with each other, which were created after the image of man, arose the God who created man after His image.

The question as to the origin of religion is not answered. It is identical with that other as to the origin of the thought of God. We cannot see how the thought of God could be the result of man's contemplation of the world, of his dim consciousness of laws and order in it. We have no analogy for this; we may watch the development in the stream of the spirit-life, and nowhere in its course does it wash up this pearl upon the bank. On the contrary, always and everywhere comes the thought of God before us as a presupposition of the thought and interpretation of the universe. God stands over against the world; there is a world above (Überwelt) which is not world, which combats the world and is combated by it. Above the world there is a something which mankind in dim surmise and recognition apprehends with fear and joy. It is inconceivable how from the world or from his own soul man should produce this thought which, in its historical realisation, ever presents itself as a gift from above. Imagine the primitive man moved by that awe before the universe that lays hold of our soul when we stand lonely over against the All; or think of his soul inspired by that breath of longing after the fountains and breasts of the All. Perhaps he came thereby to the dream of such as he in the murmuring fountain, the shady tree, the fruitful mould; but that is not God. It remains severed by an endless distance from the thought of God.

Our conceptions grow out of observations

and experiences. The world is the scene of action of these observations. But out of the mazy hieroglyphics of the world-phenomena the thought of God cannot be deciphered. Then it must be given to man from outside; from outside as the content of his soul in general comes to him from outside.

There is an old suggestive story which has the object of explaining how that happened. In the still evening hour, when the wind rustled mysteriously in the tree-tops, God walked in the garden where the first-created dwelt. The story is not history in our sense, but it gives us a solution of the problem before us in childlike, pious legend. Mankind received the thought of God, and therewith religion in that God made Himself sensible to them. There happened something external and sensuous which made necessary man's thought of the invisible God. It may be called the original revelation. Nothing more definite can be said about it, but it is not impossible, provided an operative God is assumed.

ORIGIN AND NATURE OF RELIGION 11

But never would mankind have found the thought of God from this experience, whatever the nature of it was, unless the spirit of man had been predisposed to this thought. "Man comprehends only what is in conformity to his nature," said Goethe once; otherwise expressed, there can be no religion unless man is capable of subjective religiousness.

We call a sum of conceptions and dogmas, of moral rules and institutions, of forms and formulæ, religion. But religion lives only where men experience all this as power and content of the soul. The moment a religion becomes purely objective, and this subjective element becomes extinct, the religion is dead. Religions have always died when they became purely objective—religion without religiousness.

But it can come to religiousness only if religion—above all, the thought of God—is in "conformity" with the mind. If religion were something irrational or unintelligible, it would not exist. What points of connexion has it, then, in the nature of man?

Man's relation to the world is twofold. He perceives the world as something operative and himself as purely operated on. Man, as he thinks and feels, is the last effect of that vast system of causes and effects which we call world. He is passive, absolutely dependent on the compact surrounding mass of the world-system. But, on the other hand, he stands active over against the world, setting up ends for himself and turning all that meets him to means for the realisation of those ends. He is not only operated upon, but he himself operates. As free mind he stands over against the universe and masters it. Blind action, the colossal weight of the existing, all splendour and all magnificence, all enigmas and all objects of terror—these serve for the realisation of the purposes of mind. It is precisely in our own age, an age of vast, undreamt-of mastery of the powers of nature by mind, that we understand with immediate vividness this position of man. Man as he stands over against the world, is at each moment its alpha and its omega, beginning and end. He is the result of its effects, and he is the originator of quite new effects. Such is man in his loftiness and in his lowliness: Prometheus with the fire, Prometheus with the chain!

But now the soul that feels itself dependent on what lies far below it, cries after dependence on something that is above it. And the soul that feels in itself the impulse to make tracks through the primeval forest of reality for fixed ends, strives after a very great, stable, and sure end. The soul does not find satisfaction in any kind of dependence; what it wants is to be dependent on something that lays the feeling of dependence in the deepest depths,—to be dependent on an ultimate personal Spirit. Nor is it content with all the possibilities of making roads in the primeval forest; it can do more and demands a sure goal. In the highest heights and at the furthest distance this goal must lie, if it is to bring contentment to the soul; that is, the whole impulse to action within must be released in action. Only when this has been done does the soul understand its own longing and striving thereafter; only when we know the truth do we comprehend that our unrest before was the seeking after truth; only when there comes into us the life of the Spirit from above do we understand that the Spirit from above is necessary for us, because we are spirit.

And now there lays hold of the life of the soul a power which it feels immediately as the absolute power of spirit; and before the eye that looks searchingly into the distance there rises a goal gigantic yet perceptible, impossible yet possible, above our power yet ours. Man feels the power of God, and this authority sets and gives him a goal which releases the spiritual power in him, and strains it to the utmost, and which precisely on that account satisfies.

That is religion. It is always a gift and always a task. As the God, so the gift; and as the gift, so the task. God gives the gift and with it the task. Their forms change, but the experience of the power of the Deity and the submission to it is common to all. There is a difference drawn between nature religions, moral or legal religions, and redemptive religions. It may be made clear on this customary division what we mean. In the nature religions the Deity is more powerful than man, but changeful and capricious as he; is operative in the production of purely natural gifts, such as fruitfulness and success in war, and sets therefore only such tasks as fall in the sphere of natural life. In the moral religion the Deity is overwhelmingly powerful, exalted above nature, just in character, giving men the moral laws, and thereby setting them the task of obediently fulfilling precepts, morals, rites and customs. In the redemptive religion the Deity is almighty, or is the all-operative power that out of love redeems mankind, that frees the soul from the pressure and service of the world, and thereby moves it to eternal tasks and ends above the world. The world above has laid hold upon the soul.

We have defined the nature of religion and understood that its nature corresponds to the nature of our spirit. Hence religion can become religiousness. The purpose of religion is not to lower, not to destroy and annul our free spirit-life, but to give us that life, or raise it to its perfection. Our spirit cries after religion; our nature needs religion.

But no religion without religiousness. Religiousness is the power and the life of religion.

LECTURE II

THE RELIGIONS OF MANKIND AND THE ABSOLUTE RELIGION

THE results of the former lecture may be gathered up in a few short sentences. Religious thoughts, above all the conception of God, are not innate in the mind of man. But the human mind is naturally capacitated for religion, because it is made for religiousness: in the first place, so far as it requires a supernatural, spiritual, and almighty Being in whom the disposition to dependence finds satisfaction; and secondly, in so far as it needs a final supramundane goal for the exertion of its activity. The conception of God ennobles the dependence of man, and the supramundane goal regulates the impulse towards an end.

It lies quite beyond the scope of the present course to follow the various phases which religion and religiousness have gone through in the course of a long and excessively complicated development.

The human mind assimilates new thoughts only when it relates them to its former mental content. In general, the observation may be shown to be well founded in religion too, that the human mind was striving to bring the thought of God given to it into the closest relation to the system of the universe. Both from wish and of necessity a point of connection with the known must be found. In proportion as the vivacity of the consciousness of God disappeared and man perceived the knowable and the unknowable in the world, God was drawn into the world; whether it was that men looked on the shining stars as gods, or that they endeavoured to find the Deity in the changing life of nature—in the tender awakening of spring, the iron reign of winter, the magnificence of the starry sky or the regularity of its movement—or that they chose single objects of nature and raised them to be bearers of the divine life; or finally—here the evolution reached its height — that they felt the world-order to be divine and represented the Deity as world-spirit. But amid all these changes the consciousness remained—however much the Deity was drawn down into the world—that the Deity is not the world, but in some way or other leads an independent supramundane life, possessing powers and gifts that the world does not have. There was, finally, always a feeling of God that contained more and went deeper than the worldly symbols which were made use of to express the conceptions of the divine and represent the gods.

Along with this development there naturally took place a variety of formation in the religious life and in the moral ideals.

The process we have been considering is a marvellous one. Everywhere there is a vast increase and expansion of religious conceptions and orders. There are always new gods being found, always new means of grace being discovered, always new modes of serving the Deity coming in. These creations have an extraordinary persistence. Once there they can be eradicated only with difficulty. This fact sets one thinking that in the Christian Church no dogma has really died out.

But this enormous increase in religious matter is not seldom met in history by another movement, namely to reduce the mass to simple fundamental forms, to separate the main points from the side issues and to secure their authority. Every reformation in religion—and almost every religion that has a history experiences reformations—has such a simplification in view. When the tree in full vigour grows to the height, the old branches below often wither and die.

It was not our purpose to speak of the history of religion; still, a few words must be devoted to the close of the ancient evolution. We speak of the "fulness of the times." By

THE RELIGIONS OF MANKIND 21

this biblical expression we understand the age in which the world had become ripe to receive Christianity. We have to do with the Græco-Roman world of culture, which represents at the same time the result of the religious development of the old humanity. It is well known from history what a mixed multitude of religions bore sway at this time. But with the positive religions there contended, as is not seldom at the end of an epoch of culture, the philosophic religion of the Enlightened. Think, for example, on the eclectic philosophy of a Cicero, or the Stoic ideas of an Epictetus and a Seneca. In them the feelings of the best and the tendencies of the advancing spirits found support and foundation. They laboured to save the universal in religion, while they rejected the positive. But with the positive sank also the power of religion.

Neither the flood of ancient superstitions nor of brand-new mysteries, nor yet philosophic ideas, afforded the heart what it sought, the spirit and power, motive and goal, *peace and active energy.* A terrible fear, a restless longing and striving, goes through the time. In the ages which precede the great epochs of history the poor soul arises to make a journey through the universe. Literature voices its impressions in affecting tones. The soul had gone forth to seek after the first and the last, after God and the goal of existence. And the soul travelled from god to god, from faith to faith, from goal to goal, but what it found was not its God and not its goal.

It is not a question of "conceptions," of "doctrines," or of "systems," nor of forms and formulæ in such ages of soul hunger, but of a new attitude, and a new and living content, of the soul. In the chaos of real life that surrounds it and tears its own life with it into the whirlpool, the soul wants to attain to a firm stand where a well of living water and bread of life are to be found. It seeks a traversable path through the wall of mist before it. *It is life that the soul demands.*

And the soul could not live from what the

age offered. The age was dominated by the spirit of Greece. Plato had taught to recognise the reality of the world in a cosmos of transcendent Ideas. Speculative meditation on these Ideas, spiritual contemplation of the first causes of being, was the highest meaning of life. Alongside there stood from the beginning a world of small and near ends. To do what was required by the law, the state, the order of life and piety, or particular systems of virtue, was the task of life. It is remarkable how small the world of ends of the ancients was when measured by the compass of their ideas. They had ideas, but they were poor in ideals. The highest conceptions of thought are ideas, the highest conceptions of action are ideals. Even to-day we live from the ideas of the ancients; our ideals, on the contrary, come almost entirely from Christianity.

The ideas lay far off in the transcendent fields of metaphysics: the highest point of the metaphysical pyramid was the thought of God wrapped in the mountain mists of absolute distance, lifeless, unreal. And the ideals lay so near, were so small and petty in relation to that giant pyramid of ideas, living and real, it is true, but only for the commonplace life.

But the soul needs a near God and far off ideals. The nearer the spiritual life of a person advances to us, the more powerfully are we sensitive of it, the more easily is our receptivity, the disposition to spiritual communion and inner dependence, to spiritual reception satisfied. The further the ends lie, the longer the chain of means needed for their realisation, the more powerfully and the more conformably to nature are the active powers of our soul exerted. The old world led the opposite way. God was afar off, but the ends near. Receptivity remained unsatisfied and activity retained unreleased in itself a surplus of restless, just because unexerted, powers. The soul remained fettered; the Spirit from above of which it dimly dreamt did not loose the fetters.

That was the "fulness of the times," the end of the ancient religions. When the poor soul marches through the world, then the foundations of the temples and the images of the idols on the altars, the pyramids of metaphysics and the thresholds of current morals tremble. To the "gods of Greece"[1] the soul put the question about life. They could give no answer. It was the "end of the gods of Greece."

It was at this time that a religion came forward asserting a claim which no other religion has made with such pointedness. The claim of absoluteness belongs to the very nature of religion, and is therefore wanting in none. Therewith religion always founds its claim to be the world above as against the world. But the Christian religion put forward the claim to be the *absolute religion* in opposition to all the other religions of mankind.

To realise the weight of this claim we

[1] "Die Götter Griechenlands," title of a poem by Schiller

must keep in mind a historical fact. In the Pantheon of the Roman state all religions found a place and all religions tolerated one another. Each passed for an authoritative expression of the Absolute. The Roman state was highly civilised. It did not persecute arbitrarily the confessors of religions; it was tolerant, but in spite of all tolerance it persecuted the Christians, and it did so because they asserted that they possessed the one absolute religion.

We are carried further. The question is to test the significance of this claim. It could be expressed in different forms. It could be taught that no man knows God except he to whom Christ reveals Him, or that only in the name of Jesus is there salvation for all that are on the earth or under the earth. It could be said, the gods of the heathen are demons, heathen religion and morality are immoral. Christianity could be praised as the single "sure and useful Philosophy." It was possible to teach "outside the Church no salvation," and to set the world as the kingdom of the devil over against the divine kingdom of the Church. When we look at the inner kernel, all that means the same thing.

But what was wanted, then? There was the conviction that the Christian religion is the only true one, that it alone can give peace and blessedness to all men, all ranks, all ages, all callings, all nations, all times. Christ alone makes blessed. That holds not only of the final destiny, but also of this life. Christ alone makes men perfect men, He alone gives to all peace and action. From Him alone goes forth power, happiness, life, and blessedness. "Come unto Me, ye that labour and are heavy laden, and I will give you rest." "I am the Bread of Life." "I am the Way, and the Truth, and the Life." "He that believeth on Me, though he die, yet shall he live." Christ alone is the Lord; He is the sun-hero, and all the religions of mankind are the dark cloud-dragon which He pierces through. Christianity is the tribunal over all religions, and the Christians are their judges. Nothing has real lasting worth in life apart from Christ and the service that is rendered to Him. The "imitation of Christ" is life. In His service all other ties of life may be considered small. Yes, one is to "hate father and mother" for His sake. A man's eternal destiny depends on whether he has served or resisted Him.

In this judgment there is still a final point contained. It is the conviction that Christianity cannot be surpassed; that is, that all development of the human spirit and all deep insight into the nature of the spirit and of the world will not be able to make the soul richer or to give it a new enduring standpoint. "In Christ are hid all the treasures of wisdom and knowledge"; and more than that, He is "the Life of the world." On this passage one might set forth the whole Christian religion, as we mean to do in the second part of this course and then to prove those claims of Christianity justified. But the reality of Christianity and its essential contents may be presupposed

THE RELIGIONS OF MANKIND 29

as known by all, and so the proof for the claim of Christianity can be anticipated. The particulars will be investigated later from this point of view.

These claims are enormous, and they will seem at first monstrous to many. For they mean nothing less, do they not, than that each soul remains empty and poor, without content or blessedness, crude and imperfect, that does not have thoughts of Christ and have His life for content? It is not at present our task to defend these claims, much less to give them a new interpretation. Christ was not the mild, amiable man that in many ways we make Him to-day. If anything is historically certain, it is that Christ felt Himself to be the Lord of the world, that He made the salvation of men or its opposite depend on Himself. He, He Himself was the Gospel, the new glad tidings He brought. That cannot be explained away —cannot, according to favourite apologetic manner, be toned down into the modern idea. With this claim of an unsurpassable exaltedness, and with this demand for a terrible earnestness, is Christianity come into the world, and through this demand it has conquered. We have to deal here with purely historical facts, not to pass judgment; but we do not mean to occupy ourselves with apologetics in the current sense : that can be done from very different standpoints.

But, I hear someone say, that that is historically so no one can well deny. But can the question then be discussed any further? We have so often complained of the "intolerance" of the Church; we have inwardly turned away with the feeling of the well-known Canadian from the awful fundamental proposition, "outside the Church no salvation" —and now it is said Christ thought so Himself. What confidence can we have in a man who so goes right in the face of moral tolerance?

It is said that is intolerant, and thereby it is thought much has been said, for the truth must be tolerant.

One point first of all. It was not Christ

that said, outside the organised Church, with all its dogmas and ordinances, there is no salvation, for He did not yet know such a Church. And that the opposer of the Pharisees and Sadducees with their "tradition" was no man of dogmas, of forms and formulæ, needs not to be said. Christ's view took in the whole, the first and the last. Christ made salvation dependent on communion with His person and His life. Is that an intolerance which is incompatible with truth?

What then is tolerance? There is a tolerance which grows on the basis of scepticism. Lessing's *Nathan the Wise* is the type of it. Who knows, it is said, what is truth? Every view should really be tolerated. But in reality this is not done. Lessing's judgments on the Christians in the above-named drama show that clearly. A certain kernel of truth is accepted, usually what the majority of the "educated" or the favourite science of the time looks upon as true. Sometimes it seems as if in course of time the kernel of truth would become ever smaller and smaller. With this kernel every one must agree, or he makes himself contemptible. There is no tolerance for what is considered "extreme" and "extravagant," although and because the bad conscience can never be got rid of: there might possibly be some truth in it yet!

But how, then, if someone holds, or thinks he holds, with absolute certainty a set of convictions deviating from the "ruling convictions," and if he has a real conviction? He who really has a conviction holds every opposing conviction to be false. It is here only that true tolerance can begin, the tolerance of the strongly convinced man. It rests on personal conviction, not on scepticism. Because it is only conviction that has worth—so judges this tolerance—therefore it is only conviction that can have value as conviction. Each has the right to truth, therefore to error also. No outward means of power or of persuasion may be employed to convince him. He alone can win conviction for himself, and one's own conviction alone has worth. That is moral tolerance.

This tolerance Christ exercised. As far as tolerance is concerned we cannot go against Him. But the question remains, can the above-mentioned claim of Christianity be proved? That will be the subject of the next lecture.

LECTURE III

CHRISTIANITY AS THE ABSOLUTE RELIGION

AMONG the religions of mankind Christianity occupies a peculiar place in this, that it asserts with a greater pointedness and explicitness than any other religion that it is alone and exclusively the absolute religion. A man whose word has weight among the cultured of to-day as that of scarce another, has repeated this assertion in his own way. Goethe said a few days before his end: " Let mental culture always advance, let the sciences grow in ever wider expanse and depth, and the human mind expand as it will, it will not get beyond the height and moral culture of Christianity." If one had demanded a proof from the master, perhaps he would have referred to what he had said shortly before, that it was "in his nature" to render "adoring reverence" to Christ as the "divine revelation of the highest principle of morality," as it was also "in his nature" "to revere the sun" as the mightiest "revelation of the Highest."

Or he might have fallen back on his feeling. And who will deny that a proof lies therein, namely, the proof from experience? "If any man willeth to do the will of God, he shall know of the teaching whether it be of God, or whether I speak from myself," says Christ Himself. But yet, whatever satisfaction individuals may be able to find in this, we must try, considering the extraordinary assertion we are treating of, to give another proof, or, at least, to enter upon it.

Proofs must be to a certain extent intelligible to all; they must apply standards which are accessible to everyone. But can such a proof for Christianity be produced? It is a new, exalted life that only he knows who lives it. Others have no notion of it; they talk as the blind do of colour. Christianity asserts that it alone has this life. But the other religions assert the same of themselves. In opposition to this, Christianity says that that rests on self-deception, that their life is not reality. But the reproach is returned.

We must come back on this. Let us first of all proclaim peace for to-day. We shall admit for once the reality of the content of all the religions of mankind, and ask this admission with reference to Christianity. We wish, first of all, to speak of the given thoughts under the presupposition that a reality underlies them.

Christianity is not only religiousness, but also religion. It stands as a structure of conceptions and institutions over against the systems and ordinances of the other religions. If one looks at it in this way with the eye of the historian or the philosopher, it is a religion as the other religions are. It can be compared with them, for it consists in conceptions, opinions, ideals, judgments, as they.

Now there are three standards which are applicable to all religious systems of thought. There is, first, the standard of logic; second, the standard of history; and third, the standard of the spiritual need of the soul.

The question will thus be: Is Christianity logical and consistent in its train of thought, while the other religions are inconsistent and illogical? Is that confirmed in its history? Lastly, does Christianity supply in an absolute way the need of the soul? If these questions can be answered in the affirmative, then it would be proved *that Christianity is the* RATIONAL *religion, and that it is the religion* FOR ALL, *that it is simply* THE *religion.* But that does not mean that materially it is a product of natural reason, for such products are afforded us only by pure mathematics and logic. This proposition would much rather have the meaning that historical Christianity is, formally considered, logically and rationally built up; and that, secondly, it is adequate to the deepest need of the spirit, since it accomplishes what—and more than what—the other religions promise.

He who takes a glance at the religions of mankind soon feels himself urged on to the common observation that the religious temper measures less strictly than the reason, and this is looked on as a merit. Religion is something comforting and heart-refreshing, it speaks to the heart—so it is said,—there one may not look too critically. The fragrance of religion's wondrous flower has refreshed thousands. What has fragrance to do with logic? That is well meant, and there lies an element of truth at the bottom of it also. But if one looks from the moments of elevation on the long series of thoughts and actions that fill up our life, it will not satisfy. How can the contradictory, obscure, and unintelligible satisfy in the long-run? Inconsistency and want of unity prove that foreign elements have forced their way into the organism of thought in question, that it is consequently ill, and it is even not the worst that errors have got into the truth. But to look away from that, religion threatens, with such a conception of it, to become a degenerate kind of lyric poetry.

But how can these lyrical feelings raise themselves to become principles of the human spirit, ruling and guiding life? It is neither accidental nor improper that criticism is applied to religion. The greater the weight put on a pillar, the surer must one be of its bearing capacity. The top must be secure, the bottom firm. Want of criticism does not honour religion, but depreciates it. In proportion as a religion shuts out all criticism from itself in the times of its origin, will the spiritual transformation that it introduces into humanity be accompanied by thinking; but that means by criticism as well.

We stand at a point of far-reaching meaning. There can be no question that the religions of heathendom—to characterise them shortly in a word—bear in themselves the marks of inconsistency and theoretical self-contradiction. A few examples will make this clear.

The gods claim to be served with full devotion. But other gods stand beside them and above them. And even the highest god has no absolute power at his disposal. Over the gods comes the fatal power of Moira. Arising and passing away rules among them too. The "twilight of the gods" draws near. What meaning has it, then, to serve such a god?— Prayers are required, but to them is ascribed, particularly in the form of the magic formula, absolutely sure effect. But is that possible if man nevertheless stands under the power of the gods?—Man is commanded to submit himself to the rational order of mind, whether it be the laws of the state or the social ordinances or his own reason. Sensuous nature and the vital impulses arising from it appear, on the contrary, sinful. But what sense has this command if the gods themselves are not pure spirits, if the sensuous and the spiritual have co-existed all along, and if, finally, all has gone forth from Deity?—And then religion's power of bringing blessing is praised, but deeper and deeper gloom the night-shadows of pessimism, as history shows, around the professors of religion. Religion is optimistic, but its professors are pessimists. The power of every religion is optimism, that we have from God the highest and best, and that with God we can do all things and are raised above all perils—how then can religion produce the mood of pessimism?—And finally, how may, or how can, the same mind that created and consecrated the labyrinths of superstition burst them through criticism and leave them to the curse of absurdity, and do both at the impulse of Deity?

None of this agrees with the presuppositions. The religions are irrational and inconsistent. The inadmissible is there and the impossible, and yet both come from religion.

These observations are confirmed from the history of religions. The strength of historical religions depends on the definite stage of culture. They tolerate no thoughts of one's own; enlightenment and criticism are their mortal foes. The same culture that has its roots in religion becomes in history always its judge again. It goes the opposite way from what it did with the god: the children devour the mother.

Such is the lesson of history. The religions are not absolute; they go to ruin and decay. Time and criticism become their lord. Then the moment has arrived when the holy "tradition" of yore becomes a heavy burden, which is moved painfully from one shoulder to another, or, in unguarded moments, is quietly laid aside. It is a terrible crisis. Those among us who have separated themselves inwardly from Christianity experience it similarly now in our midst. One must oneself have experienced somewhat of this misery to be able to speak of it. Life seems to be richer and simpler without religion. Religion is not an element of spiritual progress; it retards the steps and fetters hands and heart.

And then? Life pronounces its judgment. The days of religion are over, but they drag

CHRISTIANITY AS ABSOLUTE RELIGION 43

themselves on in endless succession—a heavy burden, and yet something inviolable; a hindrance, and yet "holy." Heaven makes earth a hell. The cause of religion seems lost, but no one becomes certain of his own thoughts. In this conflict the religions of mankind pass away. Not "criticism" and "unbelief" are their murderers; they die no violent death; they are themselves grown old, and new claims of the day force themselves upon the attention; those do only gravedigger services.

So the religions of heathendom grew old and died. Religion was there, but religiousness welled forth from it no more, or at any rate no strong, durable religiousness. Reason revolted against religiousness as "irrational," as untrue.

This history the Christian religion has not experienced. It has ever been the morning after the night that no evening follows. And its fields have borne their fruits, whether storm or frost passed over them. How vast are the culture transformations that it has experienced in the West! But it has also ruled them. Interests changed, all relations altered, new ideals crowded out the old, new needs arose, the reflecting mind received new tasks; but over the disappearance of old worlds and cultures, over sown and harvest fields of new worlds and new tendencies, shone clear and bright the sun of the Gospel. To the weak it transfigured weakness and gave them strength, and to the strong it ennobled strength and let them know human weakness. The strongest spirits have bowed themselves before it, and none who came to it in holy earnest did it send away with empty heart. It has passed through the ordeals of criticism smiling, and from the funeral pyres of unbelief it has risen aloft like a blessed spirit.

But, says someone, has not then Christianity, too, experienced decay, criticism, and reformation? Certainly! But it has not been destroyed by it. The decay was always conditioned, as history irrefutably shows, by the entrance of foreign elements, of "heathen" religion, or religiousness, into Christianity. The reformation consisted always in this, that the original fundamental principles of Christianity were meditated upon, or that their spiritual power led men back to them. Even in the darkest times of decline Christianity remained a power of holy Spirit. It was not Christianity that oppressed the minds in the end of the Middle Ages, but the unchristian in Christianity. Therefore religious criticism has almost always turned itself against what was not Christian in Christianity. The fundamental difference cannot be mistaken: the heathen religions succumbed to their principles; Christianity declined when it left its principles, and it revived again when it returned to them.

That is the historical contrast. But why does the human spirit always recover health again on the nature of Christianity, and why does it come to no enduring life under Paganism?

Two reasons may be given for this phenomenon. First, human reason must recognise the structure of thought of the Christian revelation as something complete in itself. Second, all the questions on which the heathen religions wrecked found here their answer. The first and last enigmas of the soul and of life were solved.

This can easily be made clear from the questions which have just been raised. He who knows God as the Almighty Love, who created heaven and earth and who penetrates all with His omnipresent will and guides all according to the norm of His Spirit, understands that this God should be served with the whole soul and with all the strength, that the fulfilling of His commands should be sought after, that He may be prayed to, not with the authority of the magic formula, but in the still and humble resignation of Christian prayer. He who feels the almighty love of this God will indeed often have the feeling of pessimism over the small and transient doings of men, but this feeling will of necessity disappear as a discord in the harmony of the optimistic faith that nevertheless all men and all events serve the last great end of existence, the Kingdom of God.

And that brings us now to the third point. Christianity satisfies the need of the human spirit. We spoke of this need in the two former lectures. It consists of two things: man needs a near, strong spiritual authority, and he needs a far-off goal. That leads the soul on to the heights of the spiritual life. Christianity gives both. Therein consists its power over souls, and therein it proves also in the highest way its "rational" character.

But does, then, the spirit of man really want authority? Have we modern men not just become free from authority through the Reformation? Does authority not seek to charm the ever-striving spirit into a rest which is quite contrary to its nature?

Certainly there is such an authority. It is external, and never comes into the heart; it does not give, but claims; it fetters the spirit, and never frees it; it kills—the death of the letter and the law is meant—and does not lead to real strong life. The spirit flees from this authority, and it should flee from it, for only spiritual stunting and dwarfing can come out of it where it persists. But it is not about this authority we are speaking. There is another freeing and living authority. It is life and power. For authority in this sense we may also say spiritual sovereignty. It is the power of the personal life that is over us, it is the depth of the Divine Spirit. This authority draws, not, however, to slavery, but to joyful, free submission; it strengthens and expands the personal life; it makes rich and not poor; it quickens and does not kill; it is of the Spirit of God and not of the letter. Such an authority man seeks from early years, for he seeks the power of the spiritual life. Think on children and on youth. It is, finally, not the "command," the "teaching," the "matter," that "captivate" us and bring us into subjection, it is the spiritual, personal Being. Not till we were "captivated" by the inspiration of a personal life over us, were we able inwardly to assimilate the teachings and matter, the commands and ordinances. And so, finally, the spirit of man finds peace only when he feels an all-encompassing and inward absolute and sure authority that gives him life for the last extremity, a life that looks death fearless in the face. This authority is the living, personal God.

The authority of God gives us two things. It transfigures our dependence on the world and its natural laws. It is not finally "force and matter," not mass and blind law, that bring our life into subjection and make it dependent. No, above all that stands, and in all that works, the living God. The dependence that we feel is finally dependence on a spiritual Person. It is only through this that it becomes bearable to the spirit and corresponds with its nature. The thousand things and experiences that oppress and limit us are

the expression of the will of God. And
limitations, like oppression, proclaim to us the
spiritual nearness of the Father in Heaven.
The God who "captivates" us breaks the
fetters of force and matter. The dependence
of our being is dependence on the Spirit of
God.

This brings us to the second point. The
God we experience gives the soul, in that we
experience Him, a goal. This goal quickens
and moves the soul to the exertion of power,
to will and to action. This goal develops all
the powers and strains them to the highest
pitch and widest compass of their possible
activity. We designate this goal "the Kingdom of God." It is a state of things where
mankind serves God willingly and from the
heart, or wills the good and does it, and thereby
has blessedness, pleasure, happiness and peace.
To bring in this state of things is the aim of
the spiritual sovereignty, or authority, of God.
But it comes about in such a manner that it
is apprehended and established by struggling,

CHRISTIANITY AS ABSOLUTE RELIGION 51

toiling humanity in the way of historical work, in gradual progress and by slow ascent, past oppositions which have been got over, or seen through and unmasked.

This end is furthered, according to the Christian view, consciously or unconsciously by all events in the world. Conscious service is the task of life. This task demands our all and gives us all in return; watchfulness over our own life, refinement and purification of the same, its exaltation and deepening, the intention to further the good and to stir up and transfigure other souls through our work and life, the constant direction of thought and action to this end.

But Christianity unites with this demand a double promise also. Firstly, the life of him who does this shall not run its course in vain and without meaning; he shall attain to worth and become a power in the great structure of events, he shall become spiritual personality and remain in all the vicissitude of the material world. And secondly, this highest exertion of power shall bring with it also the greatest satisfaction. "The doer of the word shall be blessed in his doing," says Holy Scripture.

Christianity causes men to feel the sovereignty of God, and thereby gives them the goal of the Kingdom of God. That is its essence. In the sovereignty the receptive nature of our spirit comes to rest, in the goal the active bent finds satisfaction. Both correspond to the nature of the spirit. Christianity raises the spirit to the height of the perfection attainable by it. Christianity is therefore the religion for the whole of mankind; it is the absolute and the rational religion.

What other religions promise to mankind becomes fact in Christianity alone. That promise shows that they too raise the claim to absolute truth. This presentiment is their greatness. But it remains a presentiment; no reality follows it. The dreams of the human soul become reality in Christianity: but the reality is ever other than the dream. Christianity is the test of all religions, but it

CHRISTIANITY AS ABSOLUTE RELIGION 53

is also the fulfilment of all religions. And all religions fall before Christianity, but it makes their innermost vital impulse reality. Very profoundly, therefore, all religions prove Christianity, for Christianity is *the* religion. So also it is easy to see that what was recognised in the first lecture as the nature of religion can be found again sharper and clearer in the nature of Christianity.

But he who has followed these thoughts is met finally by still another anxious question. The peace that we offered is not tenable outside in real life. Although what has been said be right, what does it avail? How if the absolute religion were only imagination? Certainly it is consistent, as castles in the air always are; and it is in conformity with the wishes of our spirit, as the pictures of phantasy always are. We stop here at the point where it is thought that the religiousness of Christianity may and should be explained as imagination. Here there is no other counter-proof than that of practical knowledge and of the experience "of the Spirit and of power." As to the reality of Christianity only he can judge who has experienced its spiritual effect. This experience is asserted by the Christians. Have they a right to make this assertion? This will be the next subject for discussion.

LECTURE IV

THE PROOF OF THE ABSOLUTE RELIGION

THE thinker is often like the hill-climber who imagines that the summit he desires to reach is close before him, but perceives to his surprise as he goes forward that hills and valleys still separate him from the final ascent. That Christianity is the absolute religion seemed to be proved by the observation of its consistency and of its relation to the spiritual need of all men. But at that point there opened before us a new ravine. Have we in Christianity realities, or only bare postulates and creations of the imagination? Is there really a God who rules over all and a Kingdom of God?

And here again lie hill and vale. Still

more weighty objections than those we mentioned may be raised. We compared Christianity with the religions of mankind. But what has such a comparison to do with the present day? It goes without saying that we do not believe in these religions. Quite other are the interests that arrest our attention. Philosophic views of the world reasoned out by great thinkers and animated by depth of spirit come upon the scene and contend with Christianity for the first place. It is these that have to be overcome, and not the paltry religions of the distant past, which at the present day run wild or wither only on the boundary line of the human species.

The magic tones of the "absolute truth" which Hegel's Philosophy tried to show to be the innate melody in the spirit of man, ever chiming forth again even out of all discords, are indeed silenced. But here Buddhism attracts, and Pessimism. The will is the essential characteristic of man, and it is his misfortune. Consciousness of the nothing-

PROOF OF THE ABSOLUTE RELIGION 57

ness of existence paralyses him gradually. That is the foretaste of blessedness, of Nirvana. There Endæmonism is praised. To advance the happiness of many brings to ourselves a moderate happiness. Again, others point us to the progress which the Evolution theory teaches. Life is not poor; in striving and struggling originate the permanent objective blessings of culture, for which it is worth while to strive whether one enjoys much or little of them oneself. And lastly, we hear from zealous adepts of the "Overman" (Übermensch). The world exists for the strong, and the strong turn it to account with ruthless mastery. The strong are right. That is fortune and truth.

And now it seems the sovereignty of God is overthrown, and the Kingdom of God perceived to be but a changing structure of cloud, resembling sometimes an angel, sometimes a man, sometimes an animal. Every man is the maker of his own fortune, his own God and Lord, the goods of this earth are his only ideals. Faust's words are true:

> "Here, on this earth, my pleasures have their sources;
> Yon sun beholds my sorrows in his courses."

And again:

> "The view beyond is barred immutably:
> A fool, who there his blinking eyes directeth,
> And o'er the clouds One like himself expecteth!
> Firm let him stand, and look around him well!
> This world means something to the capable.
> Why needs he through Eternity to wend?"[1]

Many speak so. It is not single systems, but a *practical world-philosophy* that confronts us, and we are ourselves not insusceptible to its charm. It has its followers among the upper ten thousand, and social democracy has seen to it that the lower classes also shall be thoroughly familiar with its results.

In presence of this fact, must we apply ourselves to asking for toleration, must we beg the right of existence for our faith for children and old people, for the intellectually barren and backward? Who will despise

[1] Trans. slightly altered from Bayard Taylor.

them? They too are a power! But if that were actually our situation, what could we offer to mankind as a whole? Our day would be past. It would be really the wisest policy to throw our books into the fire, and instead of audaciously demanding the highest price for the last book, to smuggle it away somehow into the Religious-history Library, that at least something of Christianity might remain or seem to remain.

But we have not come to such a pass yet, and, if we are right with what has already been laid down, we can never come to it, for Christianity is the absolute religion.

Now, then, we must acknowledge that all those ideas and ideals, however "modern" they may be, however loud their praises may sound, do not accomplish what Christianity accomplishes—they do not satisfy the hungry soul. To express it otherwise, the need of the human spirit remains, in spite of those promises and gifts, directed to the blessings of the Christian religion. "Anima naturaliter Christiana" (the soul is by nature Christian) are the words of one who knew human nature well, in presence of the terrible spiritual struggle between Christianity and Paganism in the second century of our era.

There are two questions which we must bring to bear on the above-mentioned views. Are they adequate to the practical need of the soul, which we have recognised? And secondly, are they justified in the face of theoretical reason?

The natural order of things, it is said, produces goods in its evolution and brings happiness. We may acknowledge both, but the question—it is the question of religion—remains: What does that profit my soul? This natural order, with its evolution, places me in absolute dependence on things and persons like myself, on the sum-total of occurrences. But this dependence never becomes really an absolute, soul-satisfying dependence: there remains the murmuring and complaining Why? A glance into the hearts of our fellow-men and into our own assures us of this. The murmuring against authority, which we know from our youth up, really shows only the unstilled longing for authority. We refuse to be subject to nature and history, for it is no inward subjection to which they force us. But we should be subject and—we want to be subject.

Further, we hear of "progress" and "happiness." It is said I should follow that path. But I do not perceive the progress, and I cannot do enough for it. My soul pines away under the small steps towards progress. And I do not experience the happiness: my doings do not lead to it either for myself or for others. Have I, then, caused more happiness than misery, more worth than worthlessness, in my life? In that way I never come near the goal. I am taught that I am a part and can therefore never grasp the whole; that can be done only by humanity in its gradual progress. But I am a whole, a world for myself, for I am a personal and rational spirit. My reason and will strive towards the whole, and yet I am told I should be content with the smallest fractions, never reach forward to the highest, never serve it directly, never feel its presence.

The need of my soul remains unsatisfied. These thoughts do not give me peace and active energy. And finally, is it not a terrible contradiction into which my mind is forced— terrible, for my life hangs on these things? Something exists, but it is not for me. But does anything exist—that surely means for me —if it is *not* for me? I must, it is said, always contemplate progress and happiness, but I shall never quite experience them, and yet I am told they bring me life and volition. Are my dreams and thoughts real? then my action and life are unreal, and, if my action and life are real, then what I think has no reality. In the want of inner union in the minds of so many modern men the weight of this contradiction can be realised: the ideals remain empty ideas, and impulses become ideals.

We must not deceive ourselves. The naturalism of the Evolution theory, in whatever form it appear, will never satisfy the need of the soul. Much less will the dream of the "Overman." Yes, we should become "Overmen"—the Christian too speaks of a new birth—more than a common specimen of the human species: we should leave the poor excuse, "Homo sum," for the "Ecce homo" of Pilate regarding Jesus, for the "Voilà un homme," as Napoleon said of Goethe. But what better are we of hearing what we all know, if wild paradoxes form the way to it, or rather are thrown in the way like stones?

Or can that chloroforming of the will in Pessimism satisfy? It cannot do it either. Man is no "dying flower," and so the comfort of Nirvana is of no avail. Man has a will, therefore the idea of ceasing to will in no way helps him. That this Pessimism lives among our people gives, it is true, the lie to that optimism we spoke of, but it does not thereby prove its own right. There is a Buddhist hymn which says:

> "Hast thou lost possession of a world?
> Be not saddened by it, it is nothing!
> Hast thou gained possession of a world?
> Rejoice not over it, it is nothing!
> Transient are the joys,
> Transient are the sorrows,
> Pass by the world: it is nothing!"

Alongside I set the words of a simple and strong Christian soul:

> "E'en should they take our life,
> Goods, honour, children, wife—
> Though all of these be gone,
> Yet nothing have they won,
> God's kingdom ours abideth!"[1]

That is it. There the refrain, "It is nothing," here the positive conclusion, "God's kingdom ours abideth."

And now we have made the descent and crossed the hills. We turn to the final ascent: is it realities that Christianity makes known to us?

[1] From Luther's hymn, "A Sure Stronghold our God is He," *The Scottish Hymnal*, 182.

There was a time—it remains for many still—when it seemed uncommonly easy to answer this question. The teachings of the Christian religion express realities, for "they are in the Bible." The Bible is word for word inspired by God. God cannot lie; therefore, what the Bible declares to be true is real. That was what was said, and long generations of Christendom were satisfied with it.

Why can we not be content with this answer at the present day? There are two decisive reasons. In the Biblical writings are confessedly to be found mistakes of the narrators and contradictions in the narratives. This need in no way confuse the pious Christian, but is fatal to that theory, for it would make God the originator of errors. But that is not the chief point. All sorts of apologetic artifices have been tried for the improvement of this state of affairs, but we cannot rest our faith on these artifices. It is, however, still more important to observe that the question cannot be answered in this way at all.

Others say, the content of Christianity is reality, because the authors of holy Scripture felt it to be so, and believed that they were inspired by God. But firstly, how do *we* know that these men were really "inspired"? If we are to found our faith on that, then we must be able to reach direct certainty of the historical fact. Secondly, as we may err at the present day in regard to the reality of Christianity, perhaps the authors of Scripture could do so too. And lastly, could not God's sovereignty have been once actually manifested, and be no more manifested now? We see one cannot get further by this way. In all questions concerning the life of the soul, the certainty of another never satisfies; the soul must have attained to certainty from personal experience in the matter.

What, then, do we call real? Everyone knows that Philosophy since Kant's day has devoted serious attention to this question.

The educated Christian cannot act as if this had not been done. It is improper to dispense with that accurateness and caution of thought in religious matters which men consider proper to apply to the smallest things of the world. We are done once for all with the naïve opinion that something is real inasmuch as it appears so to certain people, inasmuch as it is asserted. A glance at the microscope instructs us on that score, or a visit to the courts of justice, where unimpeachable witnesses say they have "seen" what other equally good witnesses declare "not to have happened."

The difficulty increases in the religious sphere, where it is properly no question of historical facts that can be "seen" and "heard," but of the reality of supersensuous things—the sovereignty of God and the Kingdom of God. There it is not sufficient to appeal to wonders and signs which once happened. We are dealing in the first place with facts which happen at present.

I call an event real when I am myself inwardly convinced of its reality. That a person loves or hates me, is powerful or clever, is for me reality, because I experience it. But we make a distinction between passing impressions and a firm conviction. How does this conviction come about? Not otherwise—to keep to our example—than that the influence of the other produces a definite feeling in me. Joy, love, thankfulness, respect, have arisen in me with regard to that person. Now if we ask, Whence comes this new content of my soul? I must answer, From the changeless effect of that person's influence. In experiencing in myself those continuous effects, I experience the other as real, and that in such a way that the nature and character of the other reveal themselves in this activity. Thus from the effect in me I experience the reality of a subject acting in that effect. We ourselves with the content of our soul, which is one with the soul itself, guarantee thus the activity and reality of the person working on us.

Every judgment as to the objective is consequently subjectively based in ourselves. That we are what we are is certainly due to the operation of the objective. But we know this objective only by starting from the subjective reality in ourselves; real existence and knowledge go the opposite way. The content comes to us from outside, we come to cognition from within. But this content consists in conceptions and perceptions which belong to history. God has revealed Himself historically in words and actions, in which we experience even to-day His real presence. By that we are pointed to the inmost experience of the Christian soul. That is what makes the Christian a Christian, distinguishing him from all other men.

To be a Christian means to have faith and to love. What a wealth of meaning and aim— even the whole of positive Christianity—is contained in these words, Faith and Love! I feel myself fully brought into subjection and thereby captivated, and thus set free for the highest activity. It is lasting experiences that make me subject and set me free. Now these effects necessarily presuppose something effective, but I cannot find this something in any of the phenomena which surround me in the world. They all subject me only in part and incite in me an activity directed to things of their own kind—things of this world. But faith is the consciousness of full submission, and love has not earthly fortune and worldly joy as its goal. The experience of my soul thus forces me to recognise a manifested absolute authority and sovereignty above the world, and to trace back the goal of my love to them. In other words, he who believes and loves has thereby become certain of the reality of the sovereignty of God and of the Kingdom of God. Only when this is so is the fact of faith and love in my soul intelligible. If I exist, so does God.

This seems to be a cold, speculative observa-

PROOF OF THE ABSOLUTE RELIGION 71

tion, a piece of Philosophy that remains as far from religion as the east is from the west. Can we really, it is asked, by this difficult process explain the exulting joy of the soul which is certain of the nearness of its God? Can we so explain the reality of those eternal possessions, for the sake of which men have fearlessly given property and life? Can we in this way be forced to it?

Yet he who gives us such an answer only shows that he has not understood the drift of the whole consideration, or at least forgotten it. It is not a question of "explaining" the origin of faith and love, or at all of "forcing" thereto. One who feels himself loved by another, or who entertains respect for that other, does not discover the love or the striking qualities of that other, or force himself to the recognition of them, by all sorts and kinds of reasoning. And just as little are our considerations meant to force anyone to God. It is not our intention to force or to explain, but to know and to "prove." If the lover doubts the love of his beloved, he has no other proof than reflection on the fact. So what we have to do is, not to produce or explain faith and love, but, by reflection on what we hold to be real, to prove and understand their reality.

We have reached the end of our travels for the present. Christianity is the absolute religion as opposed to all other religions and views of the world, and the grounds on which its adherents rest this judgment are not subjective creations of the imagination, but realities. He who believes and loves is sure of the sovereignty of God and of the Kingdom of God, and he has a well-founded right for this certainty.

On this summit we shall pause. Whether and how we can get a view of Christianity from it must be seen afterwards.

LECTURE V

FAITH AND LOVE

"THE Christian is the strange animal on earth," said Luther once. We have already heard enough about the Christian soul to enable us to understand what that means.

The Christian is no hermit and no cripple. Standing in the midst of this world, in the full enjoyment of its powers and goods, full of strong feeling for the real and the great in this world, the Christian asserts that there is something greater and more mighty than this world, and that this world is too small for the goal of human aspiration. The Christian, like the man in the legend, will serve only the strongest and go only the way that the strongest points him. And in this he knows himself one with the deepest aspiration of the spirit in history.

This assertion seems at first sight to be a terrible paradox. It sounds as if defiant feeling of power and infinite longing after love projected their giant shadows on the wall of the universe to experience in them the thrill of infinite love and holy fear.

But this paradox is reality. What we have heard of the sovereignty of God and the Kingdom of God might at first remind us of such giant shadows, yet these things are a reality in our soul. Faith corresponds to the sovereignty of God, and love corresponds to the Kingdom of God. The fact that Christian faith and Christian love exist requires and guarantees the other fact, namely, that there is a ruling Divine Will that penetrates and moves all, and that there is an end which this Will reveals to our soul. If the latter did not exist, neither would the former.

To understand this, we must, to be sure, free ourselves from the ideas of faith and love which custom and linguistic usage present to our mind.

"Faith" and "knowledge" are often opposed to each other, and certainty attributed to the latter, possibility or probability to the former. Knowledge seems strong and satisfying, faith weak and half-satisfying. One believes, when one does not know; knowledge is more, it is the comparative or superlative of faith. In these circumstances it is not strange that a certain aversion is felt to faith, and this aversion is increased when one, for example, hears it said: Christian faith consists in this, that definite, unprovable theoretical "doctrines," and old historical narratives of miraculous character, "must" be acknowledged as "true."

Then one soon experiences a "pleasant aversion," as the young Goethe once did, and throws faith aside without giving it much serious consideration. It cannot be other than startling to see how very quickly and easily many at the present day have done with faith. We hear, perhaps, of "struggles" said to have been undergone, but seek in vain for traces of them. In reality there has been no struggle. That can be clearly seen in the second and highest class pupils in our schools.

With love the case is not much different. It is true we hear men say the 13th chapter of 1st Corinthians is "exquisitely beautiful." They rejoice at marriages and find comfort at the grave in the words, "Love never faileth." But then, if they are asked more particularly what this "Christian love" really is, in but too many cases a multitude of words ill conceals the poverty of thought in the reply. Christian love is thought of as purely natural love. It is a "feeling" for another person; one wishes to make him happy, thinking in this manner to become happy oneself. One wishes to show kindness to the other, because showing kindness is pleasant for oneself also. In a word, the ideas cannot be got rid of which have been formed from the love of the sexes to each other, from the love of relations and friends, in the common meaning and range of the term.

I fear this common usage will introduce obscurity and confusion into our exposition, although we saw in the last lecture that by faith and love we evidently understand something different. There would, indeed, be nothing more absurd than to draw the abovementioned conclusions from *these* conceptions of faith and love. How foolish must our observations seem to him who has not thoroughly separated himself from this common conception of faith and love—or a statement like that of Paul's, that through faith man is justified before God! From my holding certain doctrines and narratives as true, it follows that God is my Lord; or from my rendering kindnesses to my friends, the judgment is confirmed that everything in the world serves a final goal above the world!

But, foolish as it is, one can often hear the Christian religion described in something like this way, and one can imagine how angry earnest and thoughtful men are at this. We must, therefore, keep clearly before us that the subject is directly and expressly the nature of Christian faith and Christian love in sequence on our last lecture; and owing to the importance of the question at stake for the whole development of our thought, we must not let ourselves be discouraged.

Christian faith has primarily nothing to do with theoretical dogmas or isolated miraculous events. It is not the "holding true" of a holy tradition. Faith is a purely personal experience, something that one comes to know practically and to be immediately sensible of. Its province is not memory or theoretical comprehension; theories are not its object. One may know and understand all the Church doctrines and "assent" fully to them, and still be unbelieving; and one may know very little of all these doctrines and doubt many of them, and yet be a believer. One may look upon worlds above with the eye of

FAITH AND LOVE

phantasy and discourse in glowing words of the power of faith, while all the time the spark is wanting in the heart. There is no faith there, however loudly it may be praised.

What are we to understand by this faith? We hear men speak of God, of His nature and will, of His love and His claims on us, of Christ and His redemptive work. That may often happen without effecting more than to give us a number of theoretical conceptions, which seem to us more or less probable. They remain useless, like withered leaves, or rather like old school-books stored away in the garret, which one has and yet does not have. But then there comes something new. We experience these conceptions; they become practical truths to us, active powers. That may happen at one particular moment which remains fixed in our memory, but it can also—and this is the rule—come through a quite slow and gradual experience. The result is the same. We become sensible of the living God: the Providential arrangements of our life, as well as what we have heard of God, are immediately experienced by us as the acts and operations of God. What formerly was conception is now reality; what formerly mere words is now the power of God. The Gospel is a "power of God," as the Apostle Paul says. The words that we have heard and meditated on become "in truth the words of God."

But *what* do we experience then? We experience an Almighty Will which demands us and our life. We feel a spiritual authority directed upon us that captivates us and disposes of us. We become conscious of the love of God which seeks us in spite of our sin, because God does not look upon our sin. We experience—to sum up all in a word—the sovereignty of God, and through it redemption from sin and from the world.

At first we resist this experience. It is as if a foreign body were trying to penetrate the eye of the soul; we blink and feel uncomfortable. Then we submit, inwardly overpowered by the truth of the matter. A terrible revolution of thoughts and feelings comes over us. We receive God's working in us, His will and His authority, willingly. We allow God to determine the content of our soul. We experience that God is gracious to us and that He moves and constrains us to His service. This act of receiving is faith. Faith is submission to God : it is obedience and it is trust. I assent to the will which demands me, and I trust the absolute authority to which my soul submits itself. There is nothing by which one can better illustrate what faith is than by the Lord's Prayer. The state of mind which the Lord's Prayer presupposes and expresses is faith: Thy sovereignty come, Thy will be done, forgive us our debts.

It is a similar occurrence when we are strongly influenced by a powerful and good person and become attached to that person. But the difference escapes no one. We remain in part free as regards every person, we take one thing and decline another; but here we feel ourselves quite dependent. And this dependence satisfies us, it fills our soul.

That is Christian faith. The act of receiving, inward submission, obedience, trust—that is its nature. It is directed to God and only to God, to His working and His actions. But when the soul in this way becomes aware of God, a marvellous and immeasurable change is accomplished in it. It is something quite new by which it lives and in which it is. It is new and yet old. The conceptions and terms we have already known for long, such as God, grace, forgiveness, new life. But they were mere words. Now they become realities. We feel ourselves surrounded by a world which is not our old world; the words become powers. These powers extend further and further in us and around us.

And these powers become now our real world. They lift us above ourselves, above the little desires and paltry cunning of our soul. "Our citizenship is in heaven." The power by which we live and the end for which we live are from another world.

But we are in this world, and that spiritual world lives and moves nowhere else than in the events and the progress we see, hear, and experience, and we cannot do other than seek for it in the world of reality. Everyone knows picture puzzles. At first glance, perhaps trees and houses are to be seen, but into this picture another is wrought which becomes visible only to him who looks for it. The world is the Christian's picture puzzle. He seeks and finds in its events another picture, God and the world of His almighty love. And when he has found this picture, it is quite difficult for him to find the first one again.

That is how the matter stands. He who believes feels himself surrounded by wonders —faith is always faith in the marvellous—for he feels the nearness of the all-ruling Lord and thereby sees the inflexible things of this world become pliant means in the hand of his

God. The almighty love which he experiences transforms for him his view of the world. He is sensible, not of unbending physical necessity, but of the hand of the Father who guides all things. To religious faith the dream of Joseph becomes reality: sun, moon, and stars come and serve it.

But the laws of the world remain: criticism and reflection fasten on the experience of faith. "Problems" arise, and no healthy mind can escape them. A process of comparing and adjusting takes place in the mind. We know that from our own life, and the ages of criticism which follow times of faith in history confirm it to us. Coarseness can contradict faith, so can culture; and coarseness and culture can borrow from each other also.

We hear of "cold unbelief," whether the epithet is used for praise or for blame. Cold unbelief is seldom seen in life. Unbelief is wont to make its appearance hot and passionate. Who is there that cannot call up examples in his mind? The passion of unbelief is a proof for faith. There is in unbelief far more belief than is generally thought. Whence, else, the excitement in the opposition to faith, if there were not something subjective in the heart of the unbeliever that spoke for faith?

It is reality that faith experiences. Even its opponent, unbelief, witnesses to that. The fact of faith witnesses to it. Men should not always go on acting as if faith in its fanatical enthusiasm produced enigmas, which unbelief then solved in cold blood. Even in the world as looked at with the eye of faith there remains much that is mysterious. But the greatest enigma of existence is solved by faith, for it explains the aspiration of the human spirit after an eternal world, and it gives this aspiration a fixed and sure direction.

If the world of faith be left out of account, the lesser enigmas are not solved, and the greatest one remains too. The fact of Christian piety, with all the blessing and all the power which are united with it, the mightiest exaltation of the spirit in the great epochs of our history, the victories of idealism, remain in their powerful reality great enigmas for him who does not recognise faith, and the living God as its content. These are at least realities not less real than the facts which we obtain from the observation of nature.

And when the problems of the soul arise from the contrast between the world of faith and the universally accessible world, they are soon solved for faith as such. Faith always works royally, for it deals with the whole. Since it experiences God, the whole is illumined and lighted up, for God is the light in its soul that makes the world bright—in spite of all things. To the theoretical view much in the particulars remains dark: the practical view of faith does not doubt, because it feels itself to be guided and determined by God. The world is for the unbeliever like a Hebrew text without vowel points; the believer understands the sense of this text, for he carries the vowels in himself and reads them into the consonantal text.

It is not a few more dogmas that faith gives us; it elevates our existence and puts us in touch with a new life. A change occurs which one may perhaps compare with the greatest change of natural life, when the child becomes a young man or woman. One has become like another being and feels oneself surrounded by a world of new realities. New relations and new interests, wonderful dreams, enchanting visions, a new life and frame of mind arise. It is only then we feel ourselves complete men, men as our parents were when we were born. So the soul which attains to faith feels itself thereby on the height of humanity, for it lives in the communion of the life and work of God, who created it in the image of His spirituality.

Such is the case with faith. The question as to faith is therefore the subject of our soul's history. We may become much and accomplish great things without faith, but the highest for which the soul exists is to be found only by the way of faith.

There are two touching texts about faith in the New Testament. The one comes from the mouth of an anxious father, "Lord, I believe, help Thou mine unbelief." The other was directed to Jesus by the apostles, "Increase our faith." Our life does not grow beyond these two requests, and it goes well with it when it lives and moves in them.

We recognised that the essence of faith consists in the receiving into us of the workings of God. But the receptivity in us takes place with reference to the active manifestation. Only then will it be lasting and powerful in us when it passes over into activity. Stimulations, impulses, views which we receive into us, remain ours only when they release the practical activity in us. That is true of the religious life also.

It was a spiritual Will that came over us and drew our life into communion with itself. To be in communion with a will means to experience its ends and to unite them with ours. We receive new ends when we experience

God's workings. There is no higher gift than ends. They come from the deepest in the other's life and stir up the deepest in ours. This gift becomes straightway a task for us. Now the purpose of God, which I experience immediately in myself, and which is in the same way experienced by all who are sensible of the presence of God, is salvation, blessedness, life, satisfaction. To experience God is to receive His purpose into our hearts. The blessedness and salvation of all, full unhindered life, the elevation of human existence above the earthly—that is the purpose of the soul that believes, for it is God's purpose. It is the Kingdom of God that the sovereignty of God effects. To devote oneself to this end with all the powers of the soul, to work for it and to serve it—that is to love.

Love is directed in the first place to God Himself. I serve Him with hearty will who is become my Lord and my authority. Peter was bidden show his love to Christ in feeding Christ's lambs. He who loves God will love those whom God loves. He will serve God in serving men. But he serves them that they may attain to the highest and best. He loves them really in striving that they may feel God's sovereignty and serve His Kingdom. That is "the best in the world" for him, and, staking his power and his interest on it, he sets to work conformably to and in virtue of the sovereignty of God which he has experienced, and again he busies himself—serving God, with the highest service which can be rendered to the world. The soul has experienced the blessedness of communion and of the service of God, and therefore it desires —as God has willed for it—this blessedness and greatness for all men.

To work spiritually, to promote inwardly, to elevate and widen life—that is the love of the Christian. Love is the law of the moral perfecting of spirits. It extends through the whole Christian's life and work; it ennobles and transfigures upbringing and family life, friendship and intercourse, social work and civil duty. It does not overawe and trample down, but frees and animates. It does not flatter and it does not lead astray, but it brings the truth and leads to the truth. It desires not bodies but souls, it seeks not only temporal delight but eternal satisfaction. It desires not to bind to itself but to attach to God. It uses many kinds of means for this end: earnestness as well as mildness, strictness as well as mercifulness, outward help as well as inward advancement. But, however it appears, whatever speech it uses, the aim remains the same: to win men's souls to the sovereignty of God and His service, and thereby to bring them life, happiness, and blessedness, to advance them to the highest elevation of existence.

And now that we understand what faith and love are and their inner connection, we shall see too that we were not hanging hundredweights on spiders' webs when we said: Where faith and love are, there is the sovereignty of God and the Kingdom of God. Has the mighty step been taken by a soul, the step of experiencing in the midst of this world the supramundane God and of serving Him? Then that soul may be certain of this God, His sovereignty and His Kingdom.

Well, says someone, that may be so, but what does that profit *me*? for I hear in the word "God" only an abstract term. But the truth always profits. Or is it of no profit to understand wherein the essence of Christianity really consists and what it means for millions? Is it of no profit to have heard the importance for our soul of what we should seek and receive? Of course, no man can give another faith, and therefore should not try. But it is always worth while to talk of the one marvellous thing that makes men free and strong, eternal and blessed in the midst of a decaying, transient world. And so these thoughts will be of profit to those who experience them along with us, and to those who only "hear" them.

But now let us turn to our development again. One point still remains in darkness.

It may be expressed thus: We have hitherto spoken of Christianity as a kind of philosophico-moral view of the world; or we have dealt only with subjective religiousness. Christianity is, however, a historical magnitude; it is a religion, and forms a Church. What should be, and what can be, our relation to it?

These questions can be dealt with only in part in this connection: other things must be reserved for a future explanation. In the next lecture they will be more fully treated.

LECTURE VI

CHRISTIANITY AS POSITIVE RELIGION

At the close of the last lecture the question arose, Can Christianity, as it has been up to this point described, be designated religion?

It is, to begin with, evident that the description is as yet incomplete, for a more exact consideration of the positive significance of the person of Christ in Christianity was intentionally left out of account. The thoughts of the sovereignty and Kingdom of God, of faith and love, were taken as "given" Christian thoughts, without express reflection on the fact that it is Christ who gave and gives them to mankind. That was presupposed. It is to the filling up of this gap that the question which has been raised leads.

Every religion is a positive or historical thing. It is no product of speculation, but whenever and wherever always primarily a matter of experience. Religion has a beginning and experiences a historical development. It contains definite teachings and institutions; it exists as a visible historical community, or as a Church.

The Christian religion has its beginning in Jesus Christ. This statement has a twofold significance. Jesus Christ is the first representative of the Christian religion. This one fact is sufficient to raise His person to the highest heights. It is not our talent and our actions, not our successes or failures, but that we have experienced God, that places us on the heights of humanity. Tried according to this standard, Christ becomes for our Christian view in the first instance the ideal man, who represents in Himself as something surely experienced that which raises mankind to the highest point of its being. But this greatest and best He Himself introduced into the hearts of men through the power of His life, and accomplished it in the history of humanity. He is still to-day the highest authority of Christendom. It is no accident that Jesus Christ is the one historical personality on whom mankind confers the title " Lord " without limitation, for in His words is felt to be almighty power. His words are the expression of the Divine will; in them is that power which awakes faith in us and gives it its content—we understand now what that means.

On that account the person of Christ has for us marvellous and Divine character. The primary question here is not one of " dogma," but of the experience of faith, that Jesus' words awaken faith or absolute submission: " To whom shall we go? Thou hast the words of eternal life." Jesus is Divine and marvellous, for the Spirit's almighty power is His own. Not in the realm of nature is the real home of the marvellous, but in the soul of man. Where spirit determines nature, this sphere begins; and where one spirit determines the other, we are

CHRISTIANITY AS POSITIVE RELIGION 97

at its middle point. But it is only Christ who has absolute power over spirits. As that is unique which Christ works in us, so His person stands unique in the world's history. Of other founders of religions also marvellous things are reported. But the marvellous clings to them like a robe of office, like an ornament or badge of honour. Christ's personal life and work is a marvel. Those men became great and greater through miracles. Christ is so great that the single miracles in relation to Him become small. But precisely on that account is He the only one whom we can really believe capable of miracles of every kind.

It is a barring of one's own way to understanding the matter, if one depends on this or that outward miracle and declares it possible or impossible. Both come to the same thing here. In this way one falls into the sphere of pure observation of nature. We understand the natural so far as we can grasp its laws. He who begins here naturally does not get any further than perhaps the resigned explanation, miracles may be possible. A man who can be trusted with an unprejudiced judgment in these things, Martin Luther, said: people call it "great miracles," when blind see and deaf hear, but Christ "looks upon that as greater which happens in souls," by as much as the soul is more than the body. But these great spiritual miracles happen every day, namely, in that Christ's word produces faith, gives blessedness and peace. This is the first miracle that has to be dealt with in the miracle problem. Only he who knows it understands the marvellous. One must have come into the sphere of the marvellous with the life of his soul to have the right to judge as to miracles. He who has the experience that Christ makes the powers of his soul and the whole of nature living to him does not find nature around him too strong or too great for Jesus' wonder-working power setting bounds to it. The "how" gives him little trouble. Why! this freedom from care characterises faith. However it happens that Christ works miracles, it is for faith immediately certain. The sovereignty which Christ exercises is Divine, therefore it is also all-comprehensive and all-penetrating. This judgment is, however, not got from the observation of nature, but from experiencing the power of Christ. Therefore faith does not see itself any more pointed to such proof as natural science gives. Even historical criticism affects it but slightly. Is Christ the Lord of the world? Then is His working marvellous; and in the measure that the spirit inwardly takes possession of this working, the miracle and the miracles of Christ conform themselves to it. In the particular cases the religious soul—but it must be religious—can view the prospect calmly, without fear and without biassed apologetics. It has the whole, and withstands the rationalistic impulse to break down the whole into particulars, to draw it down into the sphere of the common and profane.

We have, then, acknowledged that Jesus

is the beginner and author of the Christian religion. He is that through the thoughts and deeds which He once spoke and did.

However immediately present His will becomes to our soul, He does not speak to us to-day in other or new words as opposed to His historical revelation. Ecstatics and visionaries who saw Christ and heard His words again, could after all do nothing more than hand down His historical words, or else expositions and enlargements of them. The presence of Christ is not to be represented as the intermittent presence of a creature conditioned by space and time, but as eternal Will He becomes manifest in His historical words. In these words is eternal, omnipresent, personal life-power to-day not less active than then.

And now we understand what a mighty significance belongs to the reports of Jesus' sayings and working. They lie before us in the Gospels. But we see ourselves pointed beyond these. The mightier the immediate historical effects produced by a person are, the more

CHRISTIANITY AS POSITIVE RELIGION 101

vividly do these effects reflect the tendency and character of the person. He who wishes to understand the historical Jesus will therefore have recourse to the witnesses who came under the first unmixed effects of the spirit of Jesus. In this sense the complex of writings which we designate the New Testament comes into consideration for us as testimony to Jesus Christ.

The richer and more manifold the religious views and experiences in these writings are, the more valuable are they as sources for the original understanding of Christ. The Synoptists have not really narrated a history of Jesus—there are large gaps, chronological order is as good as wanting;—they wished rather to show by carefully selected and grouped words and actions of Jesus how He revealed the sovereignty of God on earth. In the same way, perhaps, the oldest oral instruction on the working of Christ was also arranged: the plan and divisions of this part of Christian instruction probably decided the order of the material with the Synoptists.—Paul gives expression to the conception that the historical Jesus is now "Lord" and "Spirit," the Spirit-power penetrating and ruling the universe. God has put the world under His feet; He who fills all in all exercises God's sovereignty and is the head of the Church. He is in us and we in Him.—John wishes to show that He who, as the Lord, is now the way and the truth, the light and life of the world, and He who once lived, taught, worked, suffered and died in Palestine is the same. The Eternal Word of God became flesh in this personality. John represents the earthly life of Christ, which was known to him, in the light of the religious experience and knowledge which, after the resurrection, he won from Christ and in Christ. Certainly the difference of intention and field of vision in John and the Synoptists presents the historian with many kinds of questions. But all these questions, whether they can be answered in the particulars or not, do not touch the princi-

CHRISTIANITY AS POSITIVE RELIGION 103

pal point with which we are concerned here. According to the conviction of the first generations which came under the influence of the working of Christ, this working is a lasting one. Christ lives on in divine power as the Lord of mankind. Not only John and Paul, but the Synoptists too, represent this conviction, for there is nothing more unhistorical than the assumption that the Synoptists wished to picture Christ as a kind of pious, thoughtful Rabbi. His earthly life and working, according to their opinion, was only the beginning of His working (Acts i. 1 ; Mark i. 1). But if this view of Christ is common to the New Testament writings, then it must go back to Christ Himself. The living, risen Christ instructed the disciples, so we hear in the oldest reports (and later fancies confirm the fact in their own way), as to His person and its significance. In this and in the lasting and continuous influences received from Him was rooted the *common faith of the apostolic time.* Now if one should say, " That is of course only a later view; Christ Himself did not think so," it is precisely His discourses as given by the Synoptists which teach us that, so this objection lacks all historical foundation. Even apart from the reports as to the risen Christ, it is still historically quite certain that Jesus felt Himself to be Lord and Judge of the universe, who should come again in glory, and the only revealer of God, and that He designated Himself as such. There is an interval between this judgment as to Himself and the words of His disciples, but it is only relative. From a purely historical standpoint, it is safer to minimise than to exaggerate it.

Then we may say, the experience of the first witnesses of Christ and His witness to Himself stand in a positive and inner connection with the knowledge of Christ which the long generations of history have experienced and won.

These are the fundamental thoughts of the New Testament revelation. It stands in connection with the Old Testament. Nothing higher can be said in its praise than that Jesus read it and founded His thoughts on it. In these books, which are records of a long spiritual history, there is to be seen at the same time the preparation for the thoughts of Jesus. They trained men for Christ. Think on the prophets' idea of God: Jahve, the Lord of the world, who guides the destinies of His people and of the nations in almighty love to the salvation of mankind. Try to realise the piety of the Psalms: " Whom have I in heaven but Thee? and there is none upon earth that I desire besides Thee. My flesh and my heart faileth: but God is the strength of my heart, and my portion for ever." A consideration of these thoughts enables one to grasp the educative power of the Eternal Spirit of God in these books.

The New Testament, and with it the Old, became the holy Book of Christendom. The Bible was declared to be the home of religious thoughts and their purest source.

What does that mean? It is a simple,

natural, and obvious thought. For deciding what Christianity really is, information is to be obtained from those who came under the original effect of the spirit of Christ. This spirit continued to work and works still. But the more stirring the effects of its operation became, the easier it was to mix with the expression given them in thought and word a foreign, natural, Jewish or Hellenic element. The mightier the rush of the waters through the bed of the stream, the more is the mud and sand stirred up. Perhaps that was never so strongly felt as in the Church of the second century, and we may think perhaps, by way of parallel, on the " enthusiasts " of the Reformation time. To the wild working of ecstatic spirits then, for example among Gnostics and Montanists, who, in the long run, had nothing better and deeper to say than the many " prophets " and enthusiasts in the agitated Reformation time, the Church opposed the word and tradition. " It is written " and " the tradition is " were constantly heard.

This was an action of mighty consequence. The centuries have felt its influence till the present day. There remained a firm breakwater in the Church, however violently the waves of fanaticism and hierarchy, of asceticism and flight from the world, of degradation and worldly pleasure raged. No stronger bulwark could be found than this. History has attested it. Manifold subjective experiences were opposed by objective history, natural excitement by divine revelation.

This was the position the Church took up towards the close of the second Christian century in the great struggles against the "Spirit" which the Gnostics and Montanists claimed to possess. Men upheld the authority of the Bible. They did it in their own way. The simple historical thought that only that is Christian which can justify its existence from the original records of primitive Christianity was thrust into a foreign mould. From the Greeks was borrowed the idea of an inspiration which made the authors merely the pens of the

Spirit. From the later Judaism came the inflexible idea of the Bible as a code of laws, the individual texts of which, apart from their connection with the whole, were to be looked on as legal precepts or teachings of equal value and authority, just like a compilation of paragraphs of "divine Law." It was only then that the "Canon" seemed to be binding enough.

And even in this conception and understanding of it, it brought endless blessing to seeking souls and to the growing Church. But the consequences of the error did not fail to appear, and they could not have failed to appear without the error destroying religion. Systems of doctrine were built up from single texts, theories of natural science and of philosophy were taken from the Bible and used to bolster up hierarchical sacerdotalism and its tendencies. Biblical language was used by those who stood at an infinite distance from the spirit of the Bible; judgment was pronounced on views and ideals according to the Bible, and fell itself under the judgment of the Bible; the

CHRISTIANITY AS POSITIVE RELIGION 109

divine spirit of the book was praised, but suppressed where and however it appeared in life.

Martin Luther freed us from this error. He recognised with the wonderful freedom from prejudice and the truthfulness which belong to genuine faith that the Bible, being a book which originated in the course of a long history, is on that account subject also to historical consideration, that is, to critical examination; that it can and should be authoritative only with reference to one thing, the knowledge of Jesus Christ—in other words, of the sovereignty and Kingdom of God. It is not what the Bible contains of cosmology and psychology, of metaphysics and exegesis, that is authoritative, but what the Bible says about religion. Religion is its content; and this content makes use of many means of expression just as the time and its culture brought them and used them. And with this there is a further point connected. That going back upon tradition and scripture, wholesome as it was, yet fettered religious experience. What was written and handed down was right; that through which it first wins its right, namely, personal experience, was pushed aside. Therein lay a tremendous danger. Perhaps Christianity in the second century was saved by becoming a book-religion, but every book-religion is threatened by the danger of becoming a legal religion, and every legal religion stifles religiousness. But what is religion without religiousness? Here, too, Luther saw clearly because he lived in faith. He recognised anew the right of subjective faith—of the Spirit. We experience God's revelation, and, in experiencing it or Christ, Christ becomes our Lord and the Scripture our authority.

Everyone knows how slowly this recognition of Luther's gained ground: in spite of it the Church presently returned to the old track. The old track had to be in many ways destroyed by a crude unhistorical criticism, by a puerile scepticism in union with irreligious historical theories, by an unbridled, unhis-

CHRISTIANITY AS POSITIVE RELIGION 111

torical subjectivity, ere it was recognised that Luther's way was the only practicable way. By this I do not wish in any way to give an opinion as to the historico-critical view of the Bible—what I said at first shows how far I am from that; I wish only to show how it came about that such violent means as were used were needed to give free scope to a religious understanding of the Bible.

But no opinion could be so premature as that we were in these things, so to say, over the difficulty. Even yet the old conception— it is not Luther's—finds representatives in our midst, who believe that it is a surrendering of religion to give history its right. And that lurking distrustful scepticism has not yet died out among us which rises when Biblical books and Biblical stories are spoken about, as if behind the Bible stood a band of fanatical and crafty forgers.

But it is not there that the chief difficulty lies. It is another thing, and it is the same for the book as for the matter. It is before all the question as to the reports of facts in New Testament history—for example, the birth and resurrection of Christ, and His miracles. Some discover in them sacred symbols of pious phantasy, religious projections thrown from the depth of the heart on the screen of objective reality; others think the miracles were the necessary means for breaking through the power of evil in the world. Others again look on these facts as means which God used in reference to the religiousness and spiritual condition of the age of revelation to bring in His sovereignty in the world, to accredit Christ. It would be rash to attempt a solution of these problems here — penetrating theological and historical considerations are involved. We have spoken of the miraculous in Christ, and shall come back on some of these points in speaking of the person and work of Christ. There some of the threads which we put aside at present can be taken up again.

Whatever position be taken up with reference to these problems, one point must here be attended to. He who is in earnest about the Christian religion—that is, he for whom it is the Christian religion itself, and not a mere discussion about it, that is important—should not depend on the changing critical or uncritical " results " of the theologians; and that holds of the theologians themselves in the long run. He should not wish to force an entrance by the thorn-hedge of criticism or the spiked railing of dogmatics, but should seek entrance where an open door leads him into communion with Christ. But over this door stand the words, " Come unto Me, all ye that labour and are heavy laden, and I will give you rest "; " He that believeth on Me shall live "; and " Seek ye first the Kingdom of God and His righteousness, and all these things shall be added unto you." Yes, under the sovereignty of God all things will fall to our lot. We depend upon that. Jesus Christ is the content of Scripture. In Him God's sovereignty becomes manifest, and the power of the Holy Spirit subdues men to this sovereignty, transforming them thereby to organs for the realisation of the Kingdom of God. That is the kernel of Holy Scripture.

If we look back now, we may say: It was not speculation that led us to the thoughts of the sovereignty of God and faith, the Kingdom of God and love, but we have received these positive religious fundamental ideas from the revelation of Christ. We have endeavoured, then, to understand it. Jesus Christ exercises the sovereignty of God and binds us thereby to the ideal of the Kingdom of God, and Jesus Christ works through this activity faith and love in our souls.

LECTURE VII

CHURCH DOGMA

IN stating the hindrances to faith at the present day it is usual to dwell on two points, miracle and dogma. In the last lecture the true way to a religious understanding of miracle was found.

The subject for present consideration is Dogma. Jesus Christ has revealed a new life to the world. Men experienced this life as a spiritual possession. It was an experiencing of the Divine sovereignty and a reaching forth towards the realisation and attainment of the Kingdom of God. But the spiritual life needs forms and order. Our spiritual possession subsists in no other form, than that of cohering conceptions, which are the expression of our spiritual possession.

There is a further point connected with this first one. This spiritual possession was not given to one but to many; it belonged to a community and it existed as a common possession. But what was common to all was experienced by each one individually. In this common experience its possessors discovered the highest and most precious content of history and of their soul. From that sprang practical tasks. A community arose which had to preserve and care for this possession, to transmit and expound it. That community is the Church.

But this possession subsisted in conceptions. Conceptions reflect life; but the mirror of the human spirit is not merely a mirror. It reads a connection into what is given, and then adapts it to its former spiritual content; it coins formulæ. The greater and newer a spiritual acquisition is, the more powerfully is it felt and experienced in the first instance as

CHURCH DOGMA 117

a unity and a whole. We come to know this condition in the New Testament writings with their uniform fundamental view and with the varied forms of presentation which they employ. But there follows of inward necessity a time when an endeavour is made to transform the many views and feelings into a short, concise system. We experience that in personal life, as mankind does in history. With reference to Christianity one may, for example, call to mind the oldest attempts towards such a summary in the baptismal confessions, from which the so-called Apostles' Creed arose.

When the human spirit attends to this its need, it attains indeed to greater clearness, to deeper understanding, and to firmer grasp of the matter. The spirit wins this insight, and does so in asserting it against a different understanding of the matter which seems to it false and dangerous. But it involuntarily disarranges and diminishes the given content, in these formations and oppositions. The spirit becomes clearer but at the same time poorer; it holds its possession faster, but the possession has become smaller.

That is the tragedy of human thought. It is experienced not less in studying the history of philosophic schools and religions than in a comparison of the richness of life with the scantiness of our conceptions of the experienced. One may lament over this and yet see the necessity of it. Thousands of blossoms deck the tree in spring, but only a few are changed with summer into fruit and come to ripeness in autumn. The tree would die if it brought all the germs of life to maturity. But it is different in the history of mind. There is no fading here as in the blossom on the tree. The germs of mental life live on, like the corn in the tombs of Egypt which has kept its life-power for thousands of years; and there comes a time when they too will take effect. And so it can be understood that, when the curtain falls after the single acts of the history of mind, we experience not only resignation but hope as well—resignation as to what has not come, hope that it must yet come.

This double experience is perhaps nowhere so much felt as in the study of Church History. The greater the gift, the heavier the task. The mightier the streams of blessing that pour in, the greater the lack of vessels to receive it. The truth and the life were given to men fully in Jesus Christ. A springtime blossomed such as man has never seen again, and its fragrance and life-giving power streamed through the universe as on a new creation-morning. And then—then came the history of the Church, and two thousand summers are well-nigh gone, and the blossoms of that time have not yet all become fruit. And still —things have become better, the long way has brought us nearer to the goal. There is, in spite of all retrogressions, a progress in the history of the Church also. Hence hope is stronger than resignation.

But to return to the point : we understand now why dogma had to arise. The experienced religion had to be intellectually formulated, and this need became all the more imperative the wilder and more confused the conceptions were which many entertained. In those great struggles against the Gnosis which led the Church to the conception of the canon—we spoke of it in the last lecture, —arose also the thought of a Church doctrine, of dogma or dogmas. And once the conception had been formed, it was a historical necessity to express it always more precisely and to extend it to ever wider provinces of religion.

So arose dogma in the course of a long history, so it grew to one of the mightiest forces in the life of mankind. We all feel its power, whether we understand or misunderstand, defend or oppose it.

Hence our consideration of Christianity would remain incomplete if we did not endeavour to attain to some attitude towards dogma. Our interest is in this naturally directed not to the dogmas of other Churches, but only to the dogmas which hold in the

Protestant Church, that is, to the dogmas which the Reformation put forward and to those of the ancient Church which it recognised and allowed to affect its practice.

The dogmas are not given by God, they are not revelation. Men have created them. How did dogmas come about? In the Church an error arose which many looked on as dangerous to souls, because it contradicted Christianity—for example, the mythological picture of Christ given by Arius; not as God, nor as man, but as a demi-god, a hero, was Christ represented, according to the model of heroes of old or "sons of the gods." Dogma rejects error and coins a formula to express the religious tendency of its originators. This formula is constructed with the scientific means at the command of the age in question. Worldly wise union-policy on the part of the spiritual, or even the will of the temporal, rulers has not seldom a share in the effect. So it was with the earliest dogma, the Nicene Creed.

A consideration of these thoughts makes the following three points clear:—1. Dogma arises from a particular historical situation, it is a historical necessity. This has just been dealt with. 2. The agreement of later times with the dogmas cannot have reference to the scientific, technical terminology of their formulation, since it belongs to a particular period of scientific knowledge and may and will soon be antiquated. The agreement has reference only to the *religious intention* of the dogma and the rejection of a particular opposite. So one can agree with Athanasius to this very hour in rejecting the teaching of Arius and in accepting the Divinity of Christ, because He is the Redeemer and awakes in us a new divine life. 3. No dogma of a Church can, as such, in itself, and as a matter of course be designated "right" by the members of that Church because, for example, the Church has produced it and upholds it; nor is any dogma "false" as a matter of course because it originated in old, little "enlightened" times, and because some theologians of another time attack it. In order to pass judgment searching examination is necessary, and the theologically unschooled can join only in part.

How then? Would it not be best without further investigation to cut dogma out of religion altogether? He who judges so would think only of his own subjective Christianity. But Christianity lives in a Church and cannot live otherwise; for it is a common possession, and can subsist only in conceptions, for it is proclaimed by men and accepted by thinking men. We have a catechism and hymn-book, we have a liturgy and books of devotion, we receive religious instruction and hear sermons. And in all these ways there presses into Christendom a vast, ancient treasure of Christian thoughts and conceptions, of Christian formulæ and sentiments, and in our own day this treasure still continues to press in. The primary question for the Christian is not concerned with the scientific formulæ of the dogmas, but with these quite practical things. But these things have received their stamp under the influence, and in virtue of the power of the dogmas.

To live in the Church means to stand under the dogmas, of course in the accepted sense. If we had to begin the history of Christianity now, it would be worth while pondering for a moment the thought of a Christianity "without a dogma." But much would not be gained by that. On account of the nature of the human mind, "new dogmas" would immediately arise. The new dogmas would become old dogmas, and other newer dogmas take their place beside them or oppose them. In a word, this way would soon lead into the old track again. Dogmas would just as little be avoided now, if we had to begin afresh, as in the Church of fifteen centuries ago. And, however "elastic" the dogmas were made, they must of necessity soon appear to many "inflexible" and useless. However restricted they were, so as to express only what was truly religious, the desire for " reduction " could not die out.

Dogma, then, is a historical necessity. But it is not a question of theoretical dogma as such for the simple Christian, but of catechism, hymn-book, liturgy, and sermon. And looked at in this way the matter is seen to be different from what it at first seemed to be. The Christian has not something unintelligible imposed on him as a law, but lives himself into given and concrete forms of life and thought. The soul has a life-content supplied to it in definite forms; and in the measure that it grasps this life-content, it will on its side penetrate the forms of it independently and spiritualise and individualise them.

But here an objection may be raised. How can one assimilate " inflexible " dogma, as it is always called ? If the old dogmas are to be valid, is not all mental progress of religious knowledge rendered illusory ? And does there not of necessity follow from the nature of human knowledge, precisely as regards

Christianity, a demand for progress in knowledge? Attention has already been drawn to this point in the present lecture.

But this objection rests on a strange popular misconception. The dogmas are in no way "inflexible." They are tenacious of life precisely on account of the extraordinary flexibility and elasticity which is peculiar to them. When it is understood that the very essence of every dogma is to give expression to a religious tendency, the tenacity and elasticity of dogma are not to be wondered at. A religious tendency comprehends an infinite mass of thoughts and feelings in itself; it admits of the most manifold combinations and the most divergent references within this structure of thought. So the old expression can remain. The more comprehensive the matter to which it refers and the hotter the battle of minds out of which it arises, the stronger will be, first, its tendency to endure, and, second, its capacity of making room for new knowledge.

CHURCH DOGMA 127

From this it may be seen that dogma does not hinder the deepening of religious knowledge, or at least does not need to do so. It is not the fault of dogma when that happens, but of those who represent dogma. If they are "inflexible" and incapable of acquiring new views, then they will make dogma "inflexible" too. That that really happens who can deny? But it is a misrepresentation of the real state of affairs when the dogmas are made responsible for this; that is, when a false, unevangelical, legal, literal interpretation of dogma is imposed by its interpreters and representatives. Here it is not the matter that is at fault, but the men. That the Protestant Church has made progress in religious knowledge with its dogmas, and not in spite of them, cannot be denied. What Luther offered and what Schleiermacher taught is not yet exhausted by a long way. The tasks which remain for us make us glad and proud, and we think dogma will not incapacitate us for their fulfilment.

Well, someone will say, that way of looking at it may be possible, but it is not the straight, royal road we are shown, but the crooked, thorny road of artificial "interpretation" and mental reservation. This argument never fails to make an impression on youthful spirits. One is forthwith ready to go the straight way; but before one is aware, it has become very crooked—the "interpretations" from which one fled return only in far worse form. Think of the artificially winding paths into which such a distinguished theologian as Ritschl led his readers, in which the new is made to appear as old and primitive.

But we must not be afraid of words, and least of all of catchwords. For what is history except the living through and grasping of ancient mental contents, the constant process of assimilating and deepening them in manifold new interpretations and combinations? Old matter is pressed into new forms, and old forms receive new matter. The thread is spun on in quiet development, but it is not snapped

CHURCH DOGMA 129

and knotted together. And it is not different as regards dogma, or more properly—for little weight is here laid on dogma as dogma—as regards the continuance, the interpretation, and the use of the old forms and matter of religious knowledge. "Let no one think that he has been waited for as saviour," said Goethe once.

So it is not denied that there can and should be new knowledge in Christianity. To strive always to deepen our grasp of the revelation of God in Christ is, we know, not only our right but our duty. But because we have a historical sense in thought and feeling, it is our opinion that the new knowledge comes from the old matter and has connection with the old forms. Only so can it become valuable and lasting knowledge. But that only is permanent in Christianity which the Church understands and grasps. And the Church understands and grasps only what is born of her spirit and grows out of her conceptions.

It is here at last that the conflicts of the

Church in all times and in our time too have their root. If we had only "academic theologians," one could look on at their conflict quite calmly, and an understanding would arise over the opposing "standpoints" sooner, perhaps, than was expected. But we have a Church, and that gives point to the antitheses, and sharpness to the battle of opinions. What is really of worth in theology has in the long run practical or ecclesiastical tendencies. On that account the strife must be borne, but on that account the power, too, can be kept fresh and the spirit unembittered.

But now we have found the answer to our problem. It was not a question as to a kind of philosophy of religion "without presuppositions" with which we were concerned, when we sought to define the nature of the Christian religion. What was wanted was to understand and interpret the revelation of Jesus Christ, and to carry that out in connection with the historical knowledge of the Church of Jesus Christ.

But now that we have endeavoured to come to an understanding over the preliminary questions and to prove the *truth* of the Christian religion, let us deal with the fundamental *truths* of the Christian religion in particular. What could, up to the present, be presupposed with reference to them must now be clarified. Thereby the rightness of the presuppositions will have to justify itself. This point of view must not be lost sight of in what follows. The question whether Christianity is really the true religion we have answered in the affirmative: the right to do this will, it is hoped, become ever clearer, the more concretely and exactly we come to know it in particular. We shall begin in the next lecture with the question of the Christian knowledge of God.

II

THE TRUTHS OF
THE CHRISTIAN RELIGION

LECTURE VIII

THE REVELATION OF GOD IN JESUS CHRIST

ABOUT the half of our way has already been traversed. We have treated of the nature and conception of religion, and of Christianity as the absolute religion. The thought that Christianity is the absolute religion is, as we have seen, inseparable from its history, as from its nature. So it has been and so it will remain.

Let us, however, at the beginning of a new year, enter into the particular fundamental truths of the Christian religion. We have sketched the picture in outline and boundary; now the details have to be filled in.

From the former discussions this, at least, will be clear to everyone: the first truth which has to be dealt with is God.

Is there a God? To have religion means answering this question in the affirmative. He who has religion in any way believes in a God. He can "prove" this faith, but he can prove it only to such as do not need the proof. The proof is accessible and intelligible only to believers.

In the main, at least, the "proofs" by which it is thought the existence of God can be established will be known to you. All believe in a God, it is said; therefore God exists. It is clear that this is no proof. The unbelief of the doubting questioner has already destroyed the force of it. Or, the world must have a first cause; but only he who believes in God will name this cause God. Or, the ends of the world are comprised in one supreme end: God has ordained this supreme end, and, with it, the whole order of ends. That, too, is a good thought; but yet it is a proof of the existence of God only for him who is in some way convinced of the existence of God before. Within the sphere of religion the proofs are superfluous; beyond that sphere they do not take effect.

So they may be left aside. The question on which all depends is this: How do I come to the conviction of the existence of God? or, better expressed, How do I come to the knowledge of God? The question for us is not as to a general philosophic knowledge, but as to the religious knowledge in the Christian religion.

All knowledge rests on experience and perception. Now a living spiritual being is experienced in the effects that are produced by it, through which it reveals to us its existence and nature. These are known through perception of the effects.

Two points are contained in this. A knowledge of God is subject to the conditions:—
(1) That God reveals Himself, that is, that He works, or lets Himself be experienced.
(2) To experience these effects one must open oneself to them and not put them aside, but, as far as possible, let them have free play.

In public meetings, when the proceedings are lively, the cry, "No interruptions," can often be heard. With the revelation of God, too, this cry would be only too often applicable.

Thus a knowledge of God presupposes a revelation of God. By revelation is not to be understood the disclosure of a definite sum of doctrines or dogmas. The doctrines arise only when the revelation is there, and is made the object of reflection. They are not the revelation, but follow as a consequence of the revelation. The only point is that the living God works. God's doings are His revelation. These doings of God were experienced once for the first time by definite men, but they are also continually experienced by many, who confirm what those men have said of the revelation. Consequently there is only *one* revelation, but two forms of experiencing revelation, the first experiencing of the effects of God's operation—often accompanied, in conformity with nature, by violent states of psychical and physical excitement—and the repetition of these experiences. It is usual to call only the first revelation.

We are Christians. That means we accept the revelation of God in Jesus Christ as *the* revelation of God, which we, or the Christian Church as a whole, receive from Christ and experience through Christ. Christ is the revelation of God, or He is the living "Word" in whom God makes His nature manifest to men. But this formula is not sufficient. It might be misconstrued as if Christ were only the Teacher of mankind, a kind of Christian Socrates, and so the conception of revelation which we have formed would be curtailed. Not only are God's thoughts declared and expounded by Christ, but God's will and working are carried out through Him. As He is the Word of God, so also is He God's working and God's action. "The Mouth of God" He was called by a Church Father: one might just as well talk of the Hand of God. Christ's thoughts are God's thoughts and His words are God's words. His heart and His dealings reveal God's mind and God's work.

But it may be objected that, as the world is created by God and is His work, nature, with the splendour of its phenomena and the impressiveness of its events, should be a worthier, more comprehensive revelation of God than Jesus; or, again, if God guides the history of mankind, the whole of the spiritual produce of the historical evolution of mankind should afford deeper insight into the nature of God than the *one* human life of Christ.

These objections seem very serious, but, on careful consideration, are found not to be of much weight. Certainly nature speaks, but its language is understood in a religious sense only by him who is in possession of the thought of God, and can, through the music of this thought, resolve the discords in the contemplation of nature into harmonies. The mirror of nature has reflected every image of Deity, Moloch not less than Jahve.—Or the total of man's evolution! Certainly, if it is a question of historical method, of the understanding of the laws of nature, of the technique of mastering the world, we have advanced beyond Christ. Our idea of the world is richer and our knowledge of the world more exact than it was in the time of Christ and the Apostles. That is evident. But all that does not lead us one step nearer knowledge of God. It touches the shell, but not the kernel. For the understanding of the Spirit who guides all things, and gives life, support, meaning, and goal, we know nothing better, higher, and more satisfying even at the present day than what we can listen to from the lips of Jesus, as we lean on the breast of the Son of Man.

This judgment is not to be explained or excused as a Christian way of speaking arising out of the fulness of the individual's conviction. It gives expression to a sober observation. The authority of the living God, His good and gracious will, the end that He sets before us, the moral work, the humanity and mercifulness of feeling, the best that even the cultured nations of our day know of these things, comes from Jesus Christ. He has shown mankind the divine and lived it as our example. The manifold remodellings and abridgments taken in hand on the thoughts of Jesus still prove, on maturer consideration, to be either simple expositions and applications, which bring nothing intrinsically "new"—think of our humane institutions and of the manifold forms of the exercise of charity—or degenerations, which represent not progress but only regress. To understand this, one must, to be sure, be sufficiently educated so as not to cling to the externalities of the words of Jesus, and to be able to distinguish the matter and the forms.

So now we can say Christendom is justified even at the present day in forming its idea of God from Jesus Christ. It is so truly. As once in the home life it was "Jesus" in whom the experience of the divine dawned upon us, so continually in the scripture lessons in

Church are God, His nature and His working, disclosed to us in the discourses and miracles of Jesus. "He that hath seen Me hath seen the Father," says Christ.

Now we are sufficiently prepared to raise the question, What do we learn, then, about God from the contemplation of Jesus Christ? This question takes us straight to the heart of the matter. Later on, Christ's person must be more particularly dealt with: a few remarks will suffice here.

The disposition and working of Jesus Christ are characterised by three things. "My Father worketh even until now, and I work." Christ is restlessly active, and His activity is uninterruptedly devoted to the salvation or the sovereignty over and redemption of mankind. We see the Teacher who never tires in making hearts sensible of God's authority by word and deed. We think of the Good Physician who without resting continues His help till deep in the night, and in giving help in bodily need never forgets to minister to the soul as well. We contemplate the Lord as He treads the path of death, steadfast and sure, because it is evident to Him that it is necessary for the salvation of mankind. This disposition and this working are the first point. It is mercifulness and *love*. To make men strong and happy, healthy and capable, to give them joy, contentment, humility, patience, steadfastness, obedience, and purpose in life—that was Christ's disposition, His working and His life.

This leads us to the second point. He is not of the world and He does not serve the world: He feels Himself independent of the limits which it sets, He fears not its blame and seeks not its praise. He is not of worldly nature and worldly character, but He is *holy*. The modern ambiguity in the meaning of this word must be got rid of in order to apply it to Jesus. In the forcible original signification holiness denotes exaltedness over the world. Holy is he whom the power of the world does not outwardly move and whom its nature does not inwardly determine.—This brings us to a

REVELATION OF GOD IN JESUS CHRIST

third point. Jesus' holy will is *almighty*. Christ makes men's hearts subject to Himself, and He rules over the order of nature. He is the Lord and He is marvellous. That belongs to His nature : it is not something that can be added or be wanting. He, and He alone, wins from the hearts of men the faith which remains steadfast in need and death. Legions of angels stand at His service. What He has now begun He will complete; falling stars and melting elements will then lie in His path. He is Lord of the hearts of men and of the world-order.

To gather these three points together: Jesus' disposition and Jesus' will, as He becomes manifest in His working in word and deed, is holy, almighty love-energy. He is the highest authority of mankind, which works faith in the heart, and He gives and realises the supreme end of the Kingdom of God, which awakens love in the soul.

Therewith is Christ's nature known. This is at the same time knowledge of God. The

God who is revealed to us in Christ is holy, almighty love-will.

Yet the question before us is not thereby answered. Whatever position be taken up with regard to the union of the divine and human in Christ, this much is clear, that the works of Christ of which we have spoken were always at the same time human works which happened within the limits of space and time. He grew tired through His constant work. He esteemed the world and death as nothing, yet experienced their power and their terrors. His might was boundless, yet He was held by the limits of arrest and cross, nails and scourging. Certainly He overcame these limits. In nothing is the divine in Christ so deeply felt as in this victory in defeat. But still the limits were there. To form a right conception of God we must look away from all these limits. We must conceive a spiritual Volition that is independent of human limitation; in other words, we must free the nature of Christ which we know from the particular

REVELATION OF GOD IN JESUS CHRIST 147

and narrow human and historical framework in which it at first revealed itself. For that purpose we shall add nothing new and foreign to the knowledge which we get in Christ, but only so express this knowledge as it must be expressed in reference to God instead of to the " God-man." The divine in Christ is the absolute love-energy. This divine is experienced by the Christian as all-ruling and all-penetrating, as the absolute power over the world. In thinking of it so, he thinks God. Let us follow, then, exactly the sketch we have made.

There is a Power which is spiritual Will, which rules the whole world. This Power is not world and no part of the world; it is not transient and changeable like the world, but holy and therein remaining like itself. God remains the same towards men in His nature and working, for He is not world. All that is has been created by this Power, for it rules the universe in an absolute manner. Everything that comes into existence is guided by it. Everything is of this Power and exists through it and has its goal in it. This spiritual Will is God, the Lord of the world. He created the world and gave it the laws of its stability; He rules in the events of this world. He created man what he is, and He makes him what he becomes. He gave man the Spirit, and He leads him on to the height of the spiritual life. The omnipotence of God asserts not only "that He can make all things," but much rather that He does make all things.

We observe the iron laws of the evolution of the world and wonder at the free development of the spirit of man, which in a slow process of evolution advances to the mastering of the existence of the world and to the experiencing of ever deeper meanings and ever richer ends of existence. But all this— whether it be the product of natural forces or the result of the struggle between manifold ideals and free strivings, is ultimately nothing else than the work of the Lord of the world. The order of nature does not stand against Him as an enemy, but represents the columns and chains which His power builds in the world. The progress of the spirit of man does not shake His throne, but is the accomplishment of the Will that rules on that throne. The spiritual freedom which man reaches is no stolen fire, but the gracious gift of the light from above. What is, is through God's will; what comes to be is through His will, and what happens serves therefore His ends. There is no motion of nature and no movement of the soul which God does not work. Where effects are, there is He; where life is, there is the living God. "Of Him and through Him and to Him are all things," says the Apostle Paul. These are not high-flying paradoxes, but expressions of the soul that has found its Lord.

The world is not "godless"; nature and history are not deprived of the Divine. This world is not a machine which moves of itself when once set in motion; it is a living thing, and lives from God and through God. But

God is never world, for He is the holy God.

All that is, however, only one side of the Christian faith in God. The great tree of the world does not exist to grow and bear leaves; it serves an end, namely, to bring eternal fruits to maturity. The temporal evolution serves an eternal end, the transient serves a permanent. And this permanent is the blessedness, the felicity, the spiritual exaltation and freeing of mankind. The almighty and holy Will is at the same time Love-will.

What does that mean? The Power which moves the world wills our salvation. Consider now what that signifies. The All-operative is the Salvation-working. Then the movement of the world exists for the sake of man; it serves the formation of each individual life— takes place for its blessedness. The almighty Power is at the same time Love-power. The highest all-ruling law of existence is holy Love. The deepest and strongest is operative Love.

He who experiences God knows Him so. The knowledge of God which the Christian wins in life always comprehends these three points in itself. He traces a spiritual Will which is holy and mighty to move all things ; and he experiences that this Will, in operating on the soul, elevates, sanctifies, and purifies it, that it causes life and blessedness. He who effects all things makes all things work for my blessedness, to the saving of my soul.

That is the Christian faith in God. Pure theoretical observation will deduce from this being of God special forms of existence ; it will speak of the personality and of the absoluteness of God. That has for us no further interest, for it is a matter of course that we must think of the all-operative Spirit as boundless, and the loving All-spirit, as we understand it, as personal. It should be no longer necessary to ward off the common misunderstanding of thinking that with personality must be accepted at the same time some kind of physical organisation for God, much less that He has a corporeality. Even the human spiritual personality is not one with the organs and means through which it exhibits itself.

Two questions have still to be attended to. Is the assertion that God's working is the working of love tenable? And, in face of human unbelief, is the thought that God is all-operative to be maintained? The questions are intimately connected together. The fact that not all men believe—that is, come to experience God—seems to destroy the force of the judgment that God effects all things, as also to stagger the conviction that God guides all things for the salvation of men. But if the matter is looked at in this way, there is danger of leaving the ground of religious knowledge, where the question is only as to what the believer experiences and feels. As to unbelievers and for what their life serves, the believer can make only indirect statements; for in his experience, this condition is only a stage which he goes through, something which must be overcome. Nevertheless, we cannot avoid these questions; for the fact that unbelief exists is a difficulty in the way of faith—it seems simply to destroy the force of judgments of faith.

Now one thing is at anyrate clear: God's sovereignty and the experiencing of this sovereignty are two different things. The fact that many do not feel this sovereignty, and hence deny it, does not suspend the sovereignty and does not alter the judgment as to its existence which the believer has formed. But the blessedness of man depends on faith as the experiencing of the sovereignty of God. So the real question at stake is, Why do not all come to faith and thereby to blessedness?

This question, however, can be treated only after man has been considered and the possible and real relations which he bears to the sovereignty of God. This, then, is the question that must be dealt with first.

LECTURE IX

MAN FREE AND GOD ALL-OPERATIVE

WE have considered the Christian thought of God. God is personal spirit, and as such almighty love-energy. His power must be thought of as effecting all things; His love makes all things work together for the salvation of believers.

Here the problem confronts us, Why do not all believe, if God is all-operative love? The Christian looks on unbelief as sin and guilt. So the problem resolves itself into this, Why is sin possible?

To find an answer for this we must go a little further back and endeavour to come to an understanding as to the nature of man.

As starting-point we may take the obser-

MAN FREE AND GOD ALL-OPERATIVE

vation which everybody makes with regard to his nature and species. Now, everyone feels himself first of all simply as a being belonging to nature. He is a part of the world, and under its laws and ordinances. He grows and becomes old, he develops and decays. The forces of nature have power over him; infection and bacilli, the occurrences of nature, and the physical changes of his organism tell upon him and change him. He is subject in this manner as a whole to the law of "must" or natural law, for nature always uses "must" as auxiliary in its great conjugation. No part of human nature is exempt from it. Thought and will, too, or the mental life, is subject to the necessity of nature. As man must think and will—being man he cannot do otherwise—so he must follow definite laws in his thinking and willing. Logic is the natural law of the mind. It takes effect, too, in the most strange fancies and in the most individual moods. There is method even in madness, and the "car tel est mon plaisir" is subject to the laws of nature.

But another point of view takes its place alongside this one—one that is also unavoidable and given in human nature. Man knows and feels himself free, self-determining personality. He himself decides for the one thing or the other offered by the possibilities of life, he himself chooses from among the possible ends, and he determines himself to one kind of action or another. Thought and will imply self-determination. Human thought and will differentiate between the inevitable "must" and the "ought," which one can comply with only of one's own free will. But the state of things is not so as if thereby man were composed of two substantially different parts. He himself as a whole is on the one side nature, and as nature conditioned by nature; and on the other free, and as free self-determining. The whole man is in the first sense the image of the world, and in the last the image of God.

It is possible to deny the last, at least

theoretically, especially in pointing to the natural constitution of man by which his power of action and his nature are conditioned. Each becomes what his nature has fitted him for; no one can win genius or talent for himself. There are born saints and "born criminals." The same results may be deduced by starting from the thought that God is all-operative. God has determined some to this, others to that. God makes some "vessels of wrath," others "vessels of mercy," as Paul says. If the goal is determined from eternity, it seems the ways to the goal are also necessary.

So in the one way or in the other, freedom or self-determination seems to be a mere illusion through which man deceives himself as to his slavery. He dreams in his prison that he is a king with crown and sceptre, with sovereignty and kingdom. That charms him for a little time, but the waking hour brings tears.

So it is said, and these thoughts are expanded

into the world-philosophy called Determinism, which may be either materialistic or religious. But these theories always shatter on facts of the inward life which each one experiences, and through which each, even the incarnate determinist, lets his actions be determined. He reflects and considers, reproaches himself for evil deeds and is proud of his good actions. He resolves to do better next time. He gives advice and commands to others, instructs and warns, educates his children and demands the obedience of their will, which he rewards, while he punishes disobedience. If life be deprived of the idea of freedom, nine-tenths of our action and thought is absurd and meaningless. The best that we do and think reckons with freedom in ourselves and in others.

To betake oneself, in view of these facts, to the hypothesis of Indeterminism, namely, that the will is not determined by anything except its own volition, would be to get from bad to worse. The assertion that our will is determined by nothing, not only destroys all religion, but contradicts as well the simplest observations which may be made on the influence of rational deliberation or of good principles on the will, on the power of habits or on the effects of racial genius, of the spirit of the time, etc., on whole groups of mankind.

Both these "solutions" explain nothing. They go to wreck on facts. Each standpoint destroys its own force in demonstrating the right of the other. It is not our task here to undertake to clarify one of the most difficult problems of philosophy with the means of philosophy. We must maintain the standpoint of Christian observation. It gives us at once two moments:—1. God is all-operative, He creates and uses men as His organs, He gives them the power to act and He brings about the success as also the scene of operations and the end in view. Every conception of God which does not contain this is of inferior value and unchristian; it sinks to the level of the naturalistic view which degrades the gods to parts of the world, to purely relative powers.

God is no more the Almighty Lord of the world, if He lets men do as they will, looks calmly on, and throws hindrances in the way only here and there when things grow too bad, or, on the other hand, when it comes to extremity, takes the obstacles out of their way. Similes of strong or weak men, of princes or lords, do not help us over the difficulty.

2. Man never acts otherwise than with the consciousness that he is acting of his own accord. The consciousness of freedom is inseparable from his inner life. If everything is given by God, so is also this consciousness of freedom and responsibility to be looked upon as God's gift, and therewith as a reality in the equipment of men.

Both these facts must be maintained, whether they can be "harmonised" or not. We may not fly the flag of the Divine power at half-mast, nor make the consciousness of freedom a shadow.

It may be shown first of all that both are a necessity for man. So far as man looks on the cosmic system and himself from the point of view of cause (causality), he must think of himself and his life and nature as caused and effected, as conditioned and dependent on the great structure of causes before him—finally on God. He is effected and therefore dependent. The more powerfully he experiences the living God, the more comprehensive and universal will this dependence show itself to him: "What hast thou that thou didst not receive?" The heroes in the history of religion —Paul, Augustine, Luther—were determinists in this sense.

But, on the other hand, man feels himself not only as end-point of what happens, but also as starting-point. He seeks out and sets aims before himself, and shapes what is suitable in the surrounding existence to means for these ends. That he does himself; he makes things far or near, real or yet to be realised, his end; he tries and chooses among means, takes those that lie ready, and extorts from nature those that are not yet to hand. In choosing an end, man raises himself above the mechanical order of nature. He makes free use of the causal order to produce a final order. The mind that wills changes the "must" around it into an "ought." It makes free use of what necessarily happens for its own end.

This is no imaginary sovereignty. Man really acts so; and the individual feels himself thereby a member of a larger community of minds which act in the same way and have the same experience, and precisely in this consciousness and in this action does he reach the summit of his existence. And the same is true of mankind as a whole; for what else is all real culture finally—I am not thinking of this or that petty invention, of the nervous pseudo-culture — than the victory of freedom over necessity, than the mastering of the causal order to further a final order? Culture is there, where the knowledge of the necessity in nature increases the power of freedom, where Tiamat, the primeval world-

MAN FREE AND GOD ALL-OPERATIVE 163

dragon of the natural forces, is conquered by Marduk, the light-god of the spirit that wills.

The causal order with its necessity is not thereby destroyed, but continues to exist. But the final order with its freedom slides itself into it and unites itself with it. Now we understand how the mind experiences the latter as well as the former on itself. Hence the latter as well as the former is reality to it. Neither can contest the existence of the other, but neither is more certain than the other. For both exist, of course, only in so far as the mind feels them, in so far as it experiences their operative power actively and passively. And it is certain that the mind experiences necessity neither less nor more than freedom. Then both are real for us and our thought.

And this result is confirmed when we place ourselves in the more precise connection of the Christian religion. It is the experience of the Christian, as we have seen, that the operative forces of the world are caused by God. The conditionality of his life is for him always at the same time dependence on God. But thereby this conditionality becomes a spiritual one. Personal Spirit effects and determines his life. In this way the innermost life and nature of the Christian are raised into the sphere of the purely spiritual. The absolute Spirit exercises His sovereignty over us and thereby directs our life to the purely spiritual goal of the Kingdom of God.

These thoughts confirm above all the feeling of dependence, ay, intensify it to the very utmost. But they elucidate and strengthen at the same time the consciousness of freedom. The more exalted above what is nearest and what is material the aims of man are, the more powerful is his feeling of freedom over against the world. When man makes the absolute goal of the Kingdom of God his own, the feeling of freedom over the system of causes of the world naturally reaches its highest pitch. Thus Christianity intensifies the consciousness of freedom. But in addition to this the Christian conception so fashions the consciousness of dependence that it can exist together with the feeling of freedom. For dependence in religion is conditioned by a spiritual Person and comes to our consciousness in the forms of intercourse with the Person. But the dependence of spiritual relationship represents itself to us psychologically as something willed and accepted by ourselves. So man can experience the absolute influences of God along with the consciousness of freedom.

But in this way the Christian religion changes the mechanical causal order into a spiritual causal order, or dependence on nature into dependence on God, and only through the latter does it make the former bearable to the spirit of man. And Christian morality brings the consciousness of freedom to the highest point in making the spirit the bearer of and fellow-worker in an absolute teleological order which surpasses all and encompasses heaven and earth. What was said before confirms itself to us here again. Christianity shows its absoluteness in intensifying the spiritual need of man to the utmost and supplying it in fullest measure. We can comprehend now how the great men of Christendom—and not only the great ones—have combined the strictest religious determinism with the highest eagerness to accomplish great things and the deepest feeling of freedom. The Apostle Paul, who testified that he had "laboured more abundantly than they all," knew that God "worketh in us both to will and to work." And Luther, whose energy endured the struggle against a world, testifies: "God has led me on like a horse whose eyes are covered so that it may not see those that run towards it." "All must happen in a maze or ignorance."

But just as little as the order of nature is destroyed by the consciousness of freedom, can the sovereignty of God be interrupted and limited. That should be clear now. But, on the other hand, God has implanted in human nature that consciousness of freedom which means there is something real in man with which and according to which he is in duty bound to reckon and act. The consciousness of duty, of guilt and responsibility, belongs to man. He demands to be judged accordingly, and has a right thereto. The idealism of some criminalists and anthropologists which is founded on materialistic determinism will not shake these facts. The guilty should receive his punishment, for the consciousness of guilt in him and the consciousness of right around him demand it. Man cannot do other than judge in this way, and indeed the deeper his moral nature is cultivated, the clearer and more distinct will this judgment be.

That should not now seem any longer enigmatic. Man "must": he must execute that whereto he is determined, and he does it. But no one is compelled to live merely in the sphere of "must"; he can feel an "ought" and he can will. Not in what he does, but in how he does it, lies its worth. Whether he acts under the pressure of a force, which may be more or less, consciously or unconsciously, natural, or himself wills, and, what is more, acts with complete self-surrender, with inward pleasure and joy, is decisive, for it is that that either leaves his character only on a level with nature or raises it into the sphere of spirituality and piety. There is a dead faith and a dead love, which come into existence in man in a purely external way without his inwardly and freely willing them; they do not change him—they leave his soul below, and do not raise it on to the heights. And there is a faith and a love in which what is most inward and tender, all the power and all the energy of the soul, pours itself forth in experiencing God Himself and serving Him. It is that that makes the soul living. Inwardness makes man what he is, and inwardness itself is freedom. That is what the hymn means:

> "Constrained by the gentle power of love,
> My soul, my all, inclines to Thee."

God effects all in us, the outward and the inward, the small and the great, and we become what He allows us to become, and that whereto He needs us. So, too, faith and love come from God into the soul. But He has so constituted us that all that happens to us becomes operative in us somehow through ourselves. Hence the question is, *how* we take and give what we must take and give. Only where the inward pleasure and joy, the spontaneity of complete devotion, draws what is given and has been stirred up within us into the heart of our own nature are faith and love really present.

It should hardly be necessary to elucidate what has been said by means of examples. A child whose duty it is to accustom itself to housekeeping and become the organ of the domestic spirit, does so because the power of influence and the force of circumstance are so strong that it simply must. But in this the child can act either mechanically and unwillingly or cheerfully and freely, and becomes inwardly poorer or richer, unhappy or happy, accordingly through its action. And every time which demands and gives great things finds many who co-operate in the work, but among them are always, according to the inward spiritual condition, many Thyrsus-bearers and few Bacchants, to use the language of Plato. "Many are called, but few chosen."

That is the answer to the question from which we started. We understand whence there is unbelief in the world in spite of the love of God.

But the objection may be raised that account has been taken only of such actions as are good, but can also be of inferior value, while there are other actions which are manifestly bad, as murder and adultery. Is it to be maintained that these, too, are effected by God? More particularly considered, however, this case only leads back to what has already been discussed. That even such actions, viewed purely as manifestations of power, go back upon God there can be no doubt. But what really makes them action and gives them moral character is something different. It is inward separation from God, aversion to what is good, unbelief and lovelessness. But that the connection of circumstances and the intensification or limitation of incentives and impulses can allow both outwardly honourable and also criminal activities to proceed from this state of the soul is of course quite intelligible. The roots are there, but, according to the nature of the soil and the condition of the surroundings, differently formed stems can grow out of them.

But why the gardener planted the one root close to a wall which obstructs it, and the other where there is plenty of open space —who could answer that, unless the gardener had told him? Or without a figure: why unbelief and lovelessness here flame up into the fire of vice, and there glimmer and smoulder as stifled flames, we do not know, for we are not able to penetrate the deepest connection in the events of this world, the last hidden causes and ends of the world-order and its evolution.

Faith brightens our life in shedding light upon the first cause and the final goal. But between these there run manifold wires under the ground, which we do not see except where they go through the house of our own life.

We have attempted to answer the question how all-operative love and unbelief can exist side by side. Here many a question may be raised. For example, we might ask why Christianity has come to many nations so late, or not at all; or one might say much in favour of the view that the question before us finds its solution still further back in the counsel of God. But time fails us to enter on these investigations, which cannot be answered in a few sentences.

These are great and serious things. One hears them only too often treated in a disposition that is paltry and blended with curiosity, anxiety, and conceit of cleverness. It is from such a disposition that the question would arise which someone put to Jesus: "Are they few that be saved?" The answer of Jesus shows us the right disposition: "Strive to enter in at the strait gate."

LECTURE X

THE NATURE OF HUMAN SIN

Nondum considerasti, quanti ponderis sit peccatum: Thou hast not considered what weight sin hath. This saying of Anselm of Canterbury is applicable to our reflections up to the present. We have pictured the sublimity of Christianity and we have been absorbed in the almighty love of God. Now the question arises: Is all that attainable by *us*?

This question may be asked with reference to the modern man with his unbelief and superstition, with his culture and the many-sidedness of his interests. Then it means: Is Christianity not too simple and too insignifiant for us, or at least a foreign flower, which could grow in the culture soil of the old world, but withers in our fields? We are beyond this old objection, for we have recognised that Christianity is so constituted that it satisfies and can satisfy the need of the human soul.

But the question raised may have still another meaning. Are we men, weak, narrow of perception, sinful, as we are and from nature cannot help being, are we capable of the life in the Spirit and of the exaltation of soul which Christianity promises and demands? Strictly speaking, this question too has been answered already in the first answer.

That is the question of the greatest men in the history of the Church. Not of the greatness and glory of the Christian religion have they doubted, but of their own power and their own nature. Think on the struggles in Augustine's soul before his conversion; think on Luther in the monastery. There the saying: "Unlearned men arise and take heaven by force, and we with our heartless erudition

THE NATURE OF HUMAN SIN 175

wallow with it in flesh and blood. Or are we ashamed to follow because others have gone before, and not ashamed at least not to follow?" "And I became dead to life." Here the despairing cry of a mortally wounded conscience, "My sin, my sin, my sin!" and the fear of being lost in spite of all the consolations and guarantees of the Church. In these struggles of the soul mankind has experienced something great. There is only one terrible and fearful thing in the world, and that is sin; and there is only one thing precious and great; it is not the world and it is not of the world; it is the power of God which becomes Lord over the sinner and sin.

Sin is the subject of our present discussion.

How do we come to the knowledge of sin? Manifestly the general outlines which we see when we look at the world are not sufficient. It is true there is wrung at last from the life of the world, from its striving and yearning, the cry of despair: "O wretched man that I am! who shall deliver me?" But this cry is drowned by the thousand voices that praise the pleasure of the world, and by the loud bustle of the day, which checks the last reflections. There are lingering diseases in which the patient feels himself relatively well and is nevertheless not well. It is their danger that they conceal themselves from the perception of the patient. Sin is such a disease. Only he who has recovered health is sensible that he has been ill. Only when the blind man formerly saw, or recovers his sight, does he comprehend the horrors of the night that surrounded him. Only he who experiences the higher life of the Spirit and the Divine grace knows that the lower life drags us down beneath ourselves and holds us there fast.

From that it follows that only the Christian can judge of the state of sin. The more inward and deep his Christianity is, the more profound will be his understanding of sin. The general complaints about sin—they fail in no age and in no human life—do not help

THE NATURE OF HUMAN SIN 177

us to the final understanding of sin. With sin it is not a question of a more or less, but of the difference between a life that is death—one does not know, says Augustine, whether this life is a dying life or a living death—and a life that is life.

Then we may say, all that makes the life of the Christian great, strong, inward, free, and happy is wanting in the life of the sinner. Sin is the contrary of what is good, and that the Christian knows. It has destroyed the good in man and always continues to destroy it, for it is the annihilation of the possession of the human soul. Sin always says No to God's thoughts and to God's will, to all that is good, true, and right. But the No is, as it were, a wheel, and the axle on which it turns says Yes. Sin says No to God because it says Yes to the empirical world with its pleasure and its life.

That may be and often is misinterpreted, as if the Christian despised and denied the world in a spirit of pietism opposed to culture and of asceticism which flees from the world. This representation of Christianity is false. What a wonderful sense of the beauty of nature; what a loving observation of men the words of Jesus disclose! How well Paul makes use of all the culture of his time! What delight Luther took in the goods and enjoyments of the natural life! We do not think on the world of nature and on the heart and mind of man when we employ the word " world" according to the usage of the Bible, but think on *the* world " which lieth in wickedness," on the world as it opposes God, on the human world as it has become in opposition to God and His will. This world assents to sin and therefore says No to God. Christianity flees from this world, not from God's world. To blame that seriously would mean praising the bad and condemning enmity against the bad.

We know wherein the essence of Christianity, as we have up to the present considered it, consists. It is faith as the experiencing of the sovereignty of God ; it is love as the service of the Kingdom of God. What contradicts this is sin, and a thing is sin only in so far as it contradicts this. So sin will be the opposite of faith and love. Or, otherwise expressed, sin is faith in the world and love to the world ; the world reigns and service is given to the world. Now it is at any rate clear what we understand by the word " world."

There is no one who does not believe in something last and highest, and who does not carry a supreme ideal in his soul. There the proofs are silent, or they are only ornament and tinsel ; there discussion ceases, investigation cannot proceed further, the first principles of the soul have been reached. And in face of all opposition the answer comes strong and simple, or defiant and disheartened : that is my " conviction."

And here the thing is decided ; here lies the difference. Some inquire after the opinions of the most prominent leading men, or listen

to the demands of the "modern" or the "old";
others follow the tendency of circumstances
and of habit, the weight of public opinion.
What they hear and what becomes their lord
is the voice of the world. The world is their
highest authority. The little street urchin
makes the strong man tremble when he can
talk in name of the "world" and mock at
him.

And if, then, out of the bustle of the day,
with its claims and business, there comes a
voice softly stealing as of an eternal authority
and power, they shut their ears, and when
the words of Christ force their way into their
hearts, they have no time. And if they must
listen, it brings them no joy and power, for
they hear with dislike and inward opposition. That is unbelief.

The blame is laid on the "doctrines" more
easily than the self-consciousness bound up
with the matter might lead us to expect.
They are declared unintelligible and unsympathetic. But it does not lie in the

THE NATURE OF HUMAN SIN 181

"doctrines"; it lies in the matter itself. The almighty authority is refused in the desire to hear the world and obey it. Where a human soul hears the eternal music of heaven and will listen, there the way to the understanding of the doctrines is easily found. It is not against the theories that unbelief turns, but against the actual experiencing of God, subjection to God, and exaltation of the soul to Him.

As one believes so he loves. For we believe at first what we afterwards love. He who experiences God in faith loves God and His purpose. He who believes in the world loves the world and its goods. These goods and the pleasure arising from them are the best thing he can strive after, for he is pointed to them by the authority he believes and the power he follows. These goods seem manifold enough. They are afforded by heaven-towering summits and still valleys; by the mountain fragrance of the mind and the vapour of sensual passion; by the Odin's oak of pride and the golden calf of riches; by things great and small, lofty and low. They bring of all sorts and therefore "something for all."

But the service they demand benefits in the long run only ourselves, and indeed only the lower and the low in us. So high-sounding the words, as low the egoism; so much pleasure, as little love. Much idealism, but no permanent great ideal; much realism, but no enduring reality to which the soul can cleave in the changing course of interests and tasks, in the alternation of hill and dale on the path of life. Pleasure in the world is in the long run always egoistic; the service of the world is finally service of ourselves alone. It is marvellous; he who does not serve God serves himself, although he wills to serve another. Man can serve only God or himself. There is no third possibility. The seeking for the third way fills a large part of the history of human idealism and—of human errors. I serve myself, but I exist for another end, and it fails;

THE NATURE OF HUMAN SIN 183

it does not compel me to its service. It is meaningless in the long run to serve the world. Pleasure in the world is egoistic pleasure.

It is marvellous, but only he who believes in God and loves Him becomes free from the ban of petty egoism. It may be seen in ordinary life that only he who is completely engrossed in an idea is able to deny himself and work not for himself alone. But the ideas of the world are not great enough to engross the whole life. It comes always ultimately to this, that the thing becomes the means and we are the end. And then it is true that whosoever would save his life shall lose it. The ends grow always smaller; they are found always more in the worthlessly individual delight; the material and particular wins the sovereignty. The soul that seeks itself loses itself. But where the Divine life penetrates us; where the absolutely Encompassing and Whole takes possession of us, there, and only there, do we become free from egoism; for there our being is incorporated as an organ in the depth of the Spirit; there we seek not ourselves, but God and His purpose. And he who loses his life in this way shall save it. "No man liveth to himself." But only he who lives in God is inwardly freed from the impulse to live, and the consciousness of living, to himself. He seeks not himself, and therefore he receives himself again an hundred-fold in the new life of the Spirit.

But what comes from this world fails. It cannot captivate us, and therefore does not satisfy us. The history of human ideals seems to afford a time when it appears possible to say to the passing moment, "Tarry, thou art so fair!" Then the ideals expire, for they are not the truth and the life. They are at the best but half truth and half life. Then the other half of the truth and the life cries out to be united with the first, that the whole may be complete. And mankind hears the cry of the other half of the truth and the life, and clutches at it to hold and save it, and so lets go the first half. Then there is rejoicing again for a little while on account of what has been found, till the cry is heard again, and again the partiality of the possession is felt. The change of opposing world-philosophies, as seen so clearly, for example, in the nineteenth century, is the judgment which they pass on one another, and is yet once more the expression of the fact that the human spirit is from the truth and for the truth. This is repeated in every individual life. Many are the attempts that are made and divers the ideals striven after; but the attempts do not still the longing, and the fruits have the worm in them. Who has not in his life experienced that with what he called " happiness "? Think of the dreams of youth. " What one wishes in youth one has in age to the full," a wise man has said. One does not attain to all happiness, but in the course of life one attains to much happiness. But it is like the " Happiness of Edenhall," or " The Ring of Polycrates."[1]

[1] " Das Glück von Edenhall," poem by Uhland; " Der Ring des Polykrates," poem by Schiller.

But even if the happiness lasts, it is not what we wished for. It is quite different from what we fondly imagined. We look at it from the distance as something absolute, which fills the whole soul — calling, work, love, social position — but on near view it becomes small and shrivels together, and the greater the expectation was, the greater the void that is left in the soul.

And yet we hold fast to what has disappointed us a thousand times, and we do not relinquish what we have found to be of naught. We make a trial with something new, although it is nearly akin to the old. We are untrue to ourselves, and delude and deceive ourselves with the illusive representation that the things we have so often found to be of naught may yet turn out to be of worth, that the flint may yet turn to gold. "They whip the mire to see if it will not become cream," says Goethe. That is the nature of sin also. And the years come and go, and the long-yearned-for happiness moves further and further off; but the sham grows and grows, as if it had really come near us. That is sin, and so is every sin constituted. It goes forth from unbelief and consists in egoistic pleasure, and asserts itself through sham. Look at the disobedient child; at the youth falling into wantonness or despondency; at the man in the centre of worldly pleasure and world-weariness; at the grey head depressed under the fear of death and impotent resignation—over all the same elements of sin determine life and lower it, and do not let it come to what it ought.

But sin is its own *punishment*. Sin is evil. That we are sinners, limits and crushes our life; it makes us sham souls and walking corpses; it holds us back from the one thing that makes us great and free. So sin is its own punishment.

But it is so in still another sense. Sin changes the whole world around us into a house of correction for us. My sin punishes the sin of others, and the sin of others punishes mine. What tortures us in life is sin, for the most grievous that befalls us arises from the badness of men and from our own badness.

And, thirdly, sin causes us to feel the oppression of the world and its system of nature fearful. Not God's upbringing, but tormenting and yet senseless enigmas are the natural sufferings of life to us, as illness, poverty, misery, death, and dying.

But there is a fourth thing that sin inflicts on us as punishment. Sin is *guilt*. To be a sinner means living in the consciousness of guilt. Thou thyself destroyest thy life; thou thyself art the gravedigger of thy happiness; thou thyself tramplest under foot thy power and thy joy; thou thyself closest thine eye against the light and life around thee; thou thyself banishest peace and active energy from thy being.

But behind this there lies another and a worse. He who sins wrongs his own being. But this being is given him by the Omnipotence which orders all things and of which everyone somehow or other has a presentiment. The soul strives as it can, and in so far as it can, against the highest it knows, to which an eternal inclination draws it. He who sins, sins against God. He is covered with guilt before God.

The measure of clearness to which men attain in this matter is different according to the religion and the morality known to them. But in every heart is somewhat of this presentiment present, so far as it feels that it has mistaken its destiny. There is a broad gulf between the words of the Psalmist, "Against Thee, Thee only have I sinned," and the dull and gloomy feeling of the ageing and pining child of the world, "O that I might begin once again; but my strength is broken and the evening is drawing near," or the superstitious illusion of the heathen, who hopes that the sacrifices offered to the Manes may still cancel the unpaid reckoning of his existence. But there is one element common to all: the consciousness of guilt, or the tormenting self-accusation that ruins one's own life. Thou thyself art guilty, thou alone! The stronger the God-consciousness is, the clearer will be the consciousness of guilt in the sinner. But even when the thought of God is dark and weak, the consciousness of guilt is not wanting. It is a new, dark, fearful enigma, in addition to all the torturing problems of existence, not one sharp sting, but a garment of stings that afflicts and galls the soul, wounds and fevers it.

That is sin, and sin is guilt. No one feels the power of sin and the sting of guilt as the Christian does; but there is no one who does not feel them.

And sin and guilt are the horror of existence. He who does not know them knows the life of the soul but poorly; and he who knows them recognises that his best is poor. He who does not know them does not know the good either; and he who knows them knows that there is nothing good in him.

That is the might of the Furies, which

ancient poetry once so powerfully painted. We no longer believe in them: they are long since forgotten. But the Furies live so long as sin lives; and sin lives so long as the heart does not experience the Deliverer of sinners. Jesus Christ is this Deliverer. Who is to have the last word in our existence? Jesus Christ or the Furies, the sovereignty of God and His forgiveness, or sin and guilt? That is the question.

LECTURE XI

Origin and Spread of Sin; the Redeemer of Sinners

Sin is evil and sin is guilt. These were the conclusions come to in our last lecture. They are justified in a certain sense by all higher religions and by all deeper philosophical tendencies. On that account they speak in common also of a redemption.

But this redemption may be understood in very different ways. It may be said, man frees himself from the fetters of his lower nature and listens to the voice of God in him: "Know thyself," that is, know the power for good in thee. That is how Socrates thought. Or one may be pointed to the heroes of mankind: they have beheld the good; follow their words of wisdom and thou shalt become free from evil. Or, finally, death may be looked upon as deliverer. When the gilded fetters of the material world break, then the spirit is set free to eternal joy in eternal light.

To all these ideas of redemption Christianity takes up a hostile attitude, not arbitrarily, but of inward necessity. Christianity has reached the deepest understanding of sin, and so needs a new conception of redemption; for in recognising the depths of sin, Christianity sees all those powers of redemption themselves holden of sin.

We must find an explanation of this fact, for only so is it possible to understand Christ as the Redeemer. We can redeem ourselves neither by good thoughts nor by good works, for "the imagination of man's heart is evil from his youth." Sin is a fundamental moral tendency in the human soul, for it is unbelief and egoistic pleasure. Not here and there in particular actions does man put the world above God; no, he desires not God at all, for he wants nothing but the world. He who rejects God and accepts the world has not God any more; he lives not to God but to the world or himself. He who denies a personal relationship, denies it completely. He who cherishes dislike, mistrust, and antipathy towards a person has inwardly broken with him. So from his side there can be no restoration of the relationship, for there is no point of connection in him from which to start. There is no self-redemption.

Neither can redemption come from the human race, for the human race is sinful as a whole. Can this be made clear? Obviously much depends on this, for it decides whether Christ is the only master, or whether it may be possible to have other masters alongside Him and even over Him.

Now, no man liveth to himself. Whether he will or not, he exists for others. His thought and will are expressed in words and actions. But words and actions produce effect. The greater and more decisive a man's thought

ORIGIN AND SPREAD OF SIN 195

and will are, the more powerful will be the effect of his influence.

There is sin in the world, and sin does not come from nature, as everyone distinctly feels who is in any degree freed from sin. If sin exists, it must have come through a man, for it belongs to the history of humanity. A man must have first committed sin, and the more this act affected his life, the more had he to show it off, and the stronger was the inducement to his fellow-men to take sides with him; for the more original an experience is, the greater the propaganda which it effects. If the universality of sin be in any degree admitted, the first sin will be dated as far back in the history of humanity as possible. The smaller the circle was then, the less the reflection and the stronger the spell of the external world, the more easily comprehensible does it become that sin spread universally. So the conclusion is arrived at that the first man was the first sinner.

That is the origin of sin, so far as it interests

us here. Thereby another point is made clear. If a man has become a sinner, he will drag mankind into his sin. What is greatest and deepest in mankind is communicated through words and deeds; but evil and sin also spread in the same way. That is the nature of social life. With this is connected a third point. Not only is man by nature adapted for the mutual effects of social intercourse: he also gives rise to a continued chain of influences. Mental tendencies are immortal. For the mind also the law of the "conservation of energy" holds good. The thought that has once been expressed and the deed that has once been done continue the effect of their influence to new generations. They build the frame in which the further life of man is lived and spin the threads which are woven into the frame.

So sin has spread and been propagated. The temperament of man afforded it ready paths to easier extension. Once there, it was like the snowflake that became an avalanche. The play of human forces in their mutual co-

ORIGIN AND SPREAD OF SIN 197

operation and opposition became sin. The mutual oppositions of men deepened sin—as seen, for example, in the story of Cain and Abel—and their co-operation spread it—as seen in the idea of the tower of Babel. The individuality of each and the manifoldness of the relations and conditions created divers shades and types of sin. Sin became individual, and character became sinful. The human type with its endless forms is not more diverse, nor all the different charms and attractions of the world more varied than sin became. The diversity of human individualities turned everything into an incentive to sin. Whatever mankind finds that is new and great has made and is making epochs also in the history of sin: for example, the discovery of America has to be mentioned in the history of sin. So sin became diverse. What a contrast between intoxicated sensuality and giddy pride, between the greed of the avaricious and the impulse of the ambitious!—and yet in their deepest nature all these phenomena are one.

That has been recognised already. But we must consider an objection which an attentive listener might possibly make here. The nature of man, it has just been said, was easily and quickly won for sin. But it was said before, the nature of man is fitted for the exaltation of soul which Christianity offers. Is not that a contradiction?

It is a contradiction, in so far as sin is certainly a contradiction not only of God, but also of the nature that has been created by God. This contradiction is, however, not unintelligible and insoluble in the particular cases. What sin affords are real goods and real emotions of pleasure. Otherwise it were unthinkable that man would take them up and persist in them. Only they are not the highest goods. But sin ever draped itself with the highest goods, as if they were robes that could be put on and off, and ever clung about culture and progress. The lower tendency always likes to gild its lowness—it was so already in Paradise—with the phrases

ORIGIN AND SPREAD OF SIN 199

"likeness to God" and "freedom," and makes itself lower thereby and testifies for all that to what is highest. Now nature, it is true, is made for the highest exertion of power. But the same nature also opposes this exertion and endeavours in the particular case always to get along with the least exertion or by the shortest way. Alongside the dry highroad there are always footpaths through the grass and mud to "cut off corners," and alongside ordinary books there are everywhere and at all times "cribs." The younger and more immature a man or mankind is, the stronger does this law of self-consideration, or the reduction of exertion, work. Thus it is quite comprehensible that mankind contented itself with smaller aims and goods, but it is just as intelligible that this condition brought no real, lasting satisfaction. But in this way, again, it is seen that Christianity is really a new creation; that it brought man to the completion of his being, and that sin hinders and limits man and drags him down under the human level.

We have seen how from the sin of the individual the sin of the race arose by spiritual connection. This thought may be confirmed through the observation of the physical propagation of the human race. This must, of course, not be understood as if generation as such were sinful; that would be, looked at theoretically, in the long run no wiser than the old rationalistic fiction that the first men were poisoned by the apple in Paradise. But if through sin man was dragged down under the human level, it must have brought about definite effects in his natural constitution. The lusts "which war against the soul" weaken and degrade the human race. In this connection mention may be made of a conception which at the present day is on everyone's lips, namely, "degeneration." But we cannot here enter on the difficult problems that are connected with the conception of "heredity." It is sufficient for us if we understand that the above-mentioned, sinful collective life of mankind, spreads all the more

ORIGIN AND SPREAD OF SIN 201

freely as the physical constitution of the human race becomes depraved through sin. The offspring of sinners became weaker, more irritable, of more " problematical nature."[1] If this coincided with the mighty mental stream of sinful tendencies which immediately enveloped the new-born child, the universality of sin became only all the more comprehensible.

But if sin is universal, then we cannot look up to any member of the human race as deliverer; they incite and lead onward, but they do not deliver.

Least of all is there any help to be got from the last possibility that was mentioned, namely, deliverance through death. He who hopes for deliverance by death surrenders the known as vain, and sets his hope of salvation on the unknown. The calculation does not tally. There remains an x, and the x is looked on as if it were a known quantity. It is not worth while to discuss this standpoint further.

[1] *Problematische Naturen*, novel by Friedrich Spielhagen.

It is mere idle talk to hold that the soul becomes happy in the unknown, while it is unhappy in the known. If the upright torch gave no light, how can it be expected to when turned upside down? The soul surely cannot, if it is to remain our ego, be transformed into something quite different after death. How can one hope to become blessed, if one does not experience blessedness? how can one await exaltation if one holds to the lower? Death delivers only him whom life has delivered: "Blessed are the dead which die in the Lord"—ay, for they lived in the Lord.

It is not we who deliver ourselves, nor does mankind deliver us, nor is death the deliverer. The human race and, with it, all its members, are subject to the curse of sin. However free they move, their movement is conditioned by the universe of action in which it now is, namely, that of sin. What lies beyond this universe of action has no existence *for them*. God's sovereignty and God's Kingdom are for

THE REDEEMER OF SINNERS 203

them no realities which urge on to decision, they are only conceptions. But conceptions do not deliver; it is the power of life that delivers.

Christianity asserts that it possesses the deliverance as the power of God unto salvation. The assertion attaches itself to the person of Jesus Christ, and to Him alone "who redeemed me, purchased and won me from all sins, from death and from the power of the devil," as our Catechism says.

Who was Jesus Christ? At first we look away from all formulæ which dogmatics have woven around His person. It is a question purely as to the historical individual.

He was born and grew up in humble circumstances. The family inheritance was small, but the national inheritance was vast. It was the conception of the sovereignty of God. God makes the new covenant of redemption: He writes the law inwardly in the heart by the almighty power of His Spirit: He forgives sin and gives to human activity the ideal of the Kingdom of God as goal. These were great thoughts. The prophet Jeremiah more than any other expressed them clearly and with effect for history. But they had become veiled and encysted in the narrow forms of national fanaticism. Babylonian metaphysics and cosmology and Hellenic philosophy had been called in to help to fashion these simple but mighty thoughts, impressively and magnificently, "in conformity with the age." Men dreamed of the destruction of the world and of new worlds, of national liberation, and of fearful judgments on the Romans and "the nations." National fanaticism was stirred up into a mighty flame, and the hopes became ever more material. And yet—there was nothing more than conceptions; and life remained small and crafty, and a paltry religiousness that thought only of reward, flourished.

Jesus experienced these great simple ideas. He felt that God was the almighty Ruler and merciful Father, He perceived the coming of His sovereignty with the most inward certainty, and saw with clear vision the Kingdom of God as the communion of the pious who serve God. He Himself was the first pious one of this nature. He lived in the consciousness of the almighty nearness of God; the need and joy of life declared to Him the sovereignty of God. He knew no other goal and no other joy than the service of the Kingdom of God. Humbly and silently He prosecuted God's cause, and with wonderful energy and power—only he who experiences them knows them—He served that end. He felt Himself to be the organ of His God, to be His servant. And this was for Him a matter of course. He made incidental use of the forms in which these things had been clothed, but they had given way under the pressure of His hand, and hung loose like a broken shell around the kernel. No break in His development, no inward catastrophe is known to us. When the Spirit moved Him to leave His retirement and enter on public life, the temptation came to Him, it is true, to unite Himself with the powers of the world so as to become master of it in that way. But He rejected it in the consciousness of serving God alone. He saw through the opposers of His work immediately, even before they had themselves become conscious of the range of their opposition. He never needed to throw away what He had honoured, and to honour what He had thrown away. The child "must be in His Father's house"; He who went to meet His death must drink the cup which the Father had prepared for Him. That is all so plain and simple, free from every hollow phrase and outward show, free from all that is won with toil and trouble and from all that is gained by one's own effort. He felt the sovereignty of God, and He served the Kingdom of God sincerely, simply, plainly, with perfectly natural self-denial. From His deepest consciousness He says, "Which of you convicteth me of sin?"

The consideration of all this might lead to the formula, Jesus was the first Christian and, in the full sense of the word, the only believer that the history of mankind knows. But over against this moment there was another, which is not less sharply and clearly impressed. The man who had come "to minister, not to be ministered unto" was at the same time conscious of being the Lord of the world. His words are God's words; He has power over all things; to believe in Him and to obey Him is the duty of man; He is the Judge of the world who shall come again in the glory of heaven. And these thoughts and claims too seem a matter of course in the mouth of Jesus. Incidentally it has again been said, Jesus is not part of the gospel which He preached. This sentence is either quite right or quite wrong. It is quite right if it means, Jesus is not related to His gospel as a part to the whole, as a paragraph to the system. It is quite wrong if its purpose is to deny that Jesus Himself is the essence and power of His gospel. He gives rest to the weary and heavy-laden; He gives life, for He is the Life. The gospel is not a "system of teaching," but the spiritual life-power of Christ.

Jesus did not need to draw special attention to these thoughts, and He did not think of excusing them. At first, His disciples did not come to the knowledge that He was the promised Messiah. But they perceived and experienced greater things in Him than had ever been expected from the Messiah. No miracle seemed to them too great, no exercise of power too world-encompassing to believe Him capable of. This impression, which lived in them, showed the wonderful power of Him by whom it was produced.

Jesus went to His death in the service of love, and in the consciousness that, dying, He was victorious. He had said before that He would rise again. The empty grave was seen by different followers, and the Risen One appeared repeatedly to the disciples. These are facts which are testified to so variously and rightly, that doubt of them can be explained only from the religious zeal of contradiction. The consciousness of the presence of the living Christ remained with the disciples even after His last appearance among them, which is called the Ascension. He lived in them and they in Him. What they had but dimly divined during His earthly life had now become clear knowledge. All the religious experience of their soul can be gathered together in the thought that He is the Lord, who now reigns and will come once again to judge the quick and the dead. But the same men did not grow weary of holding up His humility and willingness to bear suffering, His faith and His courage, as an example.

Jesus had lived—so it seems—a double life. He had felt Himself to be the Lord of the world, and He was a humble servant of the Lord of the world. So death was for Him the entrance to life, and yet it was the painful death of a poor man. And so those who believed in Him saw the man of sorrows and His humility, and nevertheless felt His sovereignty as that of Him who penetrates and guides all things.

The paradox of Jesus' self-consciousness continues through His historical position. Can a solution of it be found?

LECTURE XII

THE PERSON OF JESUS CHRIST

THERE are two historical facts which we must here endeavour to explain. How could the humblest of the children of men feel Himself to be Lord and Judge of the world, and how could the Crucified be known and adored by His followers as Lord and God? Both expressions are applied to Him in the New Testament.

As long as there are Christians both facts are recognised, and both questions have been the subject of reflection. What does history teach as to these questions? Paul and John gave expression to those facts, and the Churches founded by them did not think otherwise. For them the man Jesus, who was really and truly a man, is at the same time somehow the only-begotten Son of the Father, who had existed in heavenly glory with God, and who, after having taught, worked, suffered, died, and risen again, here below, is again in possession of divine glory and power, so that He, the Eternal, lives as Lord of His Church and rules the hearts of men.

These thoughts represent the religious faith of the Apostolic time, but they contain no theoretical answer to those questions.

The first theoretical attempt at solution was offered by the Gnostics. Jesus was something like a man, but there was much that was merely appearance in His humanity. A heavenly spirit came upon Him at His baptism and left Him again before the crucifixion, and looked on, smiling, at the wickedness of the murderers.

But it was felt that the full humanity of Jesus could not be abandoned; to explain His divine nature recourse was had to the Logos

THE PERSON OF JESUS CHRIST 213

idea. The Logos conception was current among contemporary heathen philosophers, and was a favourite word, like the conception of the "absolute," in later times. The divine reason, so it was thought, separates itself from the Godhead and enters into the world, giving it form and showing itself in human reason. The apologists of the ancient Church took over these thoughts and applied them to Christ. Hence came the idea of the "second God." Still, the unity of God could always be asserted, for God's reason is God. In Christ there are accordingly two constituent parts, the divine nature and the man Jesus, and both were embraced in the unity of *one* person.

The "second God" was for any length of time an intolerable conception. It was chiefly through the teaching of Arius that the second God became a demi-god after the pattern of Greek mythology. But there cannot be a higher and a lower God; God is of necessity one. It was the chief merit of Athanasius that he secured the recognition of this point. The one God is Father, Son, and Spirit. The Son, as also the Spirit, is the same as the Father. It is not a *like* dignity nor a *like* nature that they have, but they are one and the same God with the Father. That is the meaning of the famous word "homoousios." This conception took its rise from the working of Christ. He worked in divine power; thus He is God. But these divine operations are mediated through a genuine and complete human life; thus He is man. Since His own human life attained divine character through His God-power, He was able to invest humanity also with divine nature. So thought Athanasius.

But this creation of thought did not get beyond the character of religious assertion. As assertion it is great, for it embraces the whole matter; but as theory it remains incomprehensible—only one, yet three. But incomprehensible theories are bad, for they afford no real explanation. Hence it can be easily understood how the practical application soon took

THE PERSON OF JESUS CHRIST 215

the form: Father, Son, and Spirit are three persons, as, for example, three angels or three men; but they are one in so far as they are of like character and like nature. It was only through all kinds of artifices that this conception could be defended against the reproach of tritheism.

But the more clearly Christ was recognised as God, the greater the difficulty became when one thought of the figure of the man Jesus, which could not be forgotten. How could one unite with it the God Logos without being led to a mythological double-being? According to some the man Jesus had no human reason, its place being supplied by the Divine Logos. This was held by the opposing party to be equivalent to a denial of the humanity of Jesus: deity and humanity were two separate natures; or, according to a third party, they mingled with each other so as to form *one* common nature. The matter was not cleared up. The Council of Chalcedon, 451 A.D., decreed two natures but only one person. But how was that thinkable if both these natures are essentially personal? Recourse was had at last to the assertion that the human nature was impersonal (anhypostatic) and received personality from the divine nature, and in it and through it became personal (enhypostasia). But was, then, Christ's human nature complete; was not the result only a more or less apparent existence of the man Jesus? The God Logos is fully present, but the man Jesus exists only as a complex of human forces and capabilities. And yet the picture of Jesus was the picture of the fairest and strongest of the children of men. But wherein, if not in the personality, exist the power and the beauty of man?

The doctrine of the two natures and the one person remained, and became a "noli me tangere"; men clung to it in spite of all possible circumlocutions and new interpretations. Science changed, and there arose a new and deeper view of personality. In the time of the Church Fathers the word "person" meant individual being[1]; now the word means the mental, or spiritual nature of the individual being: the conceptions substance or nature became empty because ambiguous. But still the traditional formula was not given up; and this was right, for, as things then were, there was nothing better to put in its place, and so to give it up would have meant loss.

But what does the continuance of a formula mean? This question has already been answered. It does not mean the perpetuation of the theoretical world-philosophy and of the scientific terminology of days that are gone by, but the rejection of a spiritual tendency as irreligious and the feeling of inner union with the religious motives and the final intention of that formula. Scarcely any present-day adherent of the old formula means thereby that Christ possessed the abstract "human nature," without a spiritual human personality, or that the deity in Christ was a "substance" or a "nature." We feel and think otherwise.

[1] Einzelwesen.

For us the all-important point is that the person of the man Jesus united itself with the personal God and that thereby the man Jesus became our Lord.

No less an authority than Luther himself opened up the way to a solution. He adhered strongly to the doctrine of the two natures and the one person, and no one will suspect him of being willing to abandon anything of the divinity of Christ. But the being of God is for him not an infinite substance, but God is the personal, spiritual will of love, the almighty sovereignty of love. This eternal love-energy filled the human soul of Jesus so as to become its content. That is the divinity of Christ. Luther is vivid and rich in picturing the individual and personal life of the child and the man Jesus. But Jesus was the Lord, almighty in His love, although He restrained, concealed, as it were, His omnipotence in the days of His earthly life.

That shows us the way.

One point is at least clear. Jesus was a

THE PERSON OF JESUS CHRIST 219

man, no empty, abstract "humanity," but a real, complete man, with a powerful personal life. Jesus had a unique soul, with a peculiar mode of perception, thought, and speech. To deny that is to go directly contrary to the tradition of His life; it is simply "unscriptural."

But the content of our spiritual life is given us from outside. The will of God is the last and highest that fills our soul; but it is the will of another person, God's will, and not ours. In proportion as we are conscious of this do we feel ourselves to be organs of God and fulfillers of His will. The consciousness that we will what God wills increases in strength as time goes on. And the more we will that, the stronger does our will become, and the easier does it overcome the limitations of human skill and power, the clearer does the eye see in the intricacy of phenomena the realisation of the Divine will, and the stronger does the perception become that our life-work, too, reaches on to the final goals of existence. Fortitude unites with humility; strength is made perfect in weakness; God's will shows itself in our will; our personal life becomes a revelation of the being of God. In the ancient Church men spoke of a process by which the believing Christian was through Christ "made God."[1] Although we should not use the expression nowadays, we can understand how it arose.

But all that—it is not imagination; it is the strength and the being of our life—is broken in us by the power of sin. We share it with many others; and we share it with them because we, like them, have won it out of the fulness of Jesus Christ. More than once pious hearts have expressed the thought that we should become, as it were, "Christs," but it was always meant that we should do so through Christ, by His being "born in us."

Hence nothing could be more absurd than to put Christ on the same plane with the Christians; for what they have of likeness to Him has come from Him. The greater and stronger they were, the smaller and weaker

[1] θεοποιεῖν, Vergottung.

THE PERSON OF JESUS CHRIST 221

they felt themselves in relation to Him: He gave, and they received the best, ay, all, from His spirit. Yet these thoughts may be used as a point of connection for the understanding of the enigma of Christ's person. What we have through Him He has from God, and what takes place in us on a small scale and fragmentarily, limited and sporadic, was complete in Him.

Science starts from realities and remains science only so long as it holds this ground. But it does not merely describe the single facts; it unites them into a system. The facts themselves necessitate this; for it is not in their isolation, but as a connected whole, that they influence us. But the more extensive this system is, the greater the number of gaps for the understanding; but since we perceive it to be a unity, we endeavour to fill up the gaps. This is done by means of hypotheses. If these hypotheses hold good for the given facts, the system which they form will also be recognised as fact. Now a theory of the person of Christ can be obtained only by way of a scientific hypothesis, and this hypothesis will approach to the truth so far as it explains and unites the facts. We have ascertained the facts which are given us about Christ. Now an attempt must be made to unite them in the Christian system as a whole. For this the following hypothesis serves.

The God-will that guides the history of mankind to salvation entered into history in Jesus, became man in Him, and worked after the method of human history in His words and deeds. This special Divine will revealed in history fashioned the man Jesus as its organ and as the clear and definite expression of its being. It created the man Jesus, as once the first man, for its organ—that is the last and deepest significance of the very ancient historical tradition that Jesus was born of the Virgin Mary—and united itself with the man Jesus from the first moment of His existence; it acted on Him, and permeated His feeling, thought, and will. Thus the man Jesus became "Son of God." This designation, as it is used of the kings of Israel and also in the New Testament of the Christians ("child of God"), points, *in the first place*, only to the particular guarding and guiding Father-relation of God to the man Jesus. God was operative in the man Jesus in such a way that all the thoughts and emotions of His soul, His aspiration and will, always assented to and carried out the God-will that dwelt in Him and determined Him. "My meat is to do the will of Him that sent Me." That was His life, the content and power of His soul, and must have held good of the child and youth as well as of the man, of the teacher and wonder-worker, of Him who died and rose again. What He felt, willed, thought, said, and did, was worked in Him by the personal God-will that dwelt in Him, and stands out with all the freedom and joy, all the power and blessedness of the human soul which belongs to its God and serves Him.

By the expression "personal God-will," as it is used here and also later on, is meant not a mere operative force which proceeds from God, as it is active elsewhere also, but the Divine Person Himself. A person is nothing else than conscious personal will. The Divine Person entered so into Jesus as to become *one* spiritual personal life with Him. He worked in the human life of Jesus, not from outside inwards, not by leaps and bounds and interruptedly as in us, but from inside outwards, revealing Himself in Him and giving His thoughts, words, and actions their content and goal. All that the man Jesus thought and did was given and worked by God, who was one with Him. Nay, more, He could not look upon His thoughts otherwise than as God's thoughts; He could not will without the consciousness that God willed. His personal life was for Himself the life of God, for God was the hidden source in His soul from which went forth that which made His soul a peculiar soul. To prevent theological mis-

THE PERSON OF JESUS CHRIST

understanding it may be mentioned here that Jesus felt Himself in His personal completeness, including the God-will which had become His will, as another, a second in relation to the Father. His Divine personal will or His Divine personality was for His own consciousness the eternal Son of the Father in heaven. He was not a prophet endowed by God, according to His self-consciousness, but God, as the Father and with the Father. The Divine Person in Him was a special volition in relation to the volition of the Father. But this brings us to a new sphere, the thought of the Divine Trinity, to which we must return later on.

And yet the expression and effect of the Divine presence in Jesus during His earthly life had a limit. It was not, as with us, the limitation of sin; it was the limitation of human nature as such. The empirical sinful man must not be taken as the measure of man. It is only the measure of the idea of humanity, or of what man is to become in eternity, by which the measure of the man

Jesus can be defined. He, as man, was in this world what we hope to be in the other world, the means and organ of God, unlimited, marvellous, and boundless. Thus He knew the secrets of heaven, which remain enigmas to us, and He possessed powers which slip from our hands.

So the authorities of the day became small in His sight, this world with its honour and pleasure, with its parties and its great ones. "All things have been delivered unto Me of my Father; and no man knoweth the Son, save the Father; neither doth any know the Father, save the Son, and he to whomsoever the Son willeth to reveal Him." The living God and the eternal truth permeated His soul and formed its content. It was thus that He was able to express the heavenly in earthly wise, and yet it remained heavenly. His thoughts took shape on the small and finite, and yet they were infinite and eternal in their power and significance. It is the gift of the leading spirits in the history of religion to express the unlimited and eternal tersely, definitely, and so as to be intelligible to all. But only after great pains have they attained to this capacity, and it has frequently failed them and left precisely their best still in darkness. Jesus possessed it without limit and without struggle, for His life flowed direct from God and all things were delivered unto Him of the Father. On that account the laws of nature and the free hearts of men also submitted to the omnipotence of His love. So the earth became the footstool of His feet and heaven His throne. So He became the Lord, and the world entered His service. So legions of angels streamed to Him, and He needed them not. So He felt Himself the Lord of men till the last day, although the hatred of men drove the nails through His hands and feet.

So far as Jesus knows and feels Himself the organ of God, His Son, He is Lord of the world, for the world is God's and God is in Him. He Himself is, according to the peculiar content of His soul, God. And again, He is

God's servant, for not from His human soul as it was by nature, but from God, came the sovereignty and the power.

That is the secret of the soul of Jesus. We understand it, though we have but a dim presentiment of its meaning, for we never experience it as He. It draws us to Him, but it also casts us at His feet; it raises us above ourselves in subjecting us to Him. We receive "all" in Him, but we receive it only through Him.

Now we understand the double reference in Jesus, His glory and His humility. He was a man as we are, and God dwelt in Him and worked in Him; we experience that too. But His life and working was God's life and working, and that we never reach; for He is the Lord and we are the servants; He is the originator and we are the followers; He is God and we are men; He had it and we strive after it; but only through Him do we strive after it, and only from Him do we expect it.

One thing still must be attended to in this

connection: the significance of the resurrection of Christ. In the New Testament sense the resurrection of Christ is God's seal upon His life and work. The Jews killed Jesus, but God restored Him to life; they decided against Him, and they were stronger than He; but God was for Him, and He was stronger than they. That gives mankind the certainty that the good will conquer as it conquered in Jesus Christ. If Jesus had remained in death, the decision would have been against Him. There was no means in those days to show His disciples, His opposers, and the world that Jesus was right except His being restored to life. He who serves God lives eternally. On that account Jesus became alive again. That is a miracle; but the victory of the good is the miracle of history, however different the forms of this victory may be. That Judaism was wrong and Jesus right is established by the resurrection. Judaism lived to die and Jesus died to live. Life is God's verdict in the struggle of the opposing forces in history.

But we must not lose ourselves in the details of dogmatics. Here we must be content with the result. The man Jesus was guided by God's personal will in every moment and in every activity. Considering what the life of Jesus was, we must not conceive God's will working in Him merely as a kind of inspiration which comes and goes and is received or not. The union with God was in Jesus a lasting, fixed, and natural one. The person of God dwelt in Him and had united itself inseparably with the human volition and feeling. It was really *one* personal life that Jesus lived. The determining will of God became every moment in Him human self-determination, which never came about otherwise than as the effect of God's operation. The thoughts He had were God's thoughts of grace, but they were cast in the historical forms of the Israelitish religion. The redeeming sovereignty of God over the world, for example, took the historical form of the traditional representation of the working of the Messiah. From this may be understood the peculiar coincidence of clear, strong self-consciousness and the feeling of "must" in the soul of Jesus. His thoughts sprang from the God in His heart, and His actions came from God and were therefore wrought in His power. What is reported of them is not more wonderful than His words are. It is the words of Jesus that we are pointed to first nowadays. Signs must be seen and the force of them felt; for it is in the immediate impression that their power lies; the words take effect to-day as they did centuries ago. He who feels in them the wonderful life from God knows of the power of Jesus over the world. He who reflects further will see that the whole life of Jesus becomes intelligible from this standpoint. But not less will it be clear that the divinity of Christ in the New Testament sense is asserted here. Our hypothesis has verified itself, and it does not give us less of the divine being and the divine operation of Christ than the Ancient Church hypothesis of the two natures as it is usually expressed.

Still one point which has already been referred to needs explanation. It is quite intelligible how the human consciousness of Jesus should stand out in opposition to the heavenly Father. But Christ continues to exist in the sphere of divine glory, and is co-ordinated with the Father and the Spirit as Son. These thoughts are not later dogmas, but belong to primitive Christianity. The formula, Father, Son, and Spirit, which runs both clearly and in more hidden notes through the whole New Testament, may with moral certainty be traced back to Christ Himself. And I cannot help thinking that in this formula the conception "Son of God" had another and deeper significance than in the usual application. But this leads to a further thought; it seems as if the Divine Being of Christ too must be thought of somehow as another alongside the Father and different from Him. That cannot be taken in the sense of a demi-god, nor yet as establishing a heavenly family. That would be all mythology and unchristian polytheism. And all the sophisms by which an attempt is made to show that three can at the same time be one, must be put aside all the more, whether elements, or parts of a whole, or psychical functions, are thought of.

As far as I can see, another way must be taken. What do we experience of God's personal life from the operation of Jesus Christ? The will of God that sinners be saved, and that there be a communion of the elect in the world. But when, apart from the consideration of Christ, we look around us, we find the same almighty will operative again in nature, as also in the natural evolution of mankind therewith connected: God wills that the world exist and develop. And again, this will becomes operative in us, affecting our heart by the words of another, as the personal will that the individual souls in their particular situation and with their particular needs become God's or be saved. These sentences, strictly speaking, comprehend all that can be predicated of God. God is personal Spirit or rational operative will. God wills that the world exist and develop; God wills a history that shall lead mankind to salvation, or the rise and growth of a Church; and God wills that a multitude of particular individual souls be His.

The endless range of the Divine working shows itself in this threefold direction. God does nothing further than the work of realising these three volitional acts—or we can at least say nothing of anything beyond them.

In every conscious act of the will the entire spiritual person goes forth. With us men the different acts of the will follow each other in succession, so that while the one is consciously operative, the other sinks back into the sphere of the potential or the unconscious. But for the absolute Divine Being, such unconscious circumstances are simply unthinkable. So in the eternal God those three volitional acts, together with their realisation, are eternally co-existent. In each the whole Divine Person goes forth, and each of them differentiates itself in virtue of its particular intention and operation from the others, however much the effects of their operation coincide and are related one to another. It is the one God whom Christendom knows, one Person, who reveals Himself as the threefold Person. It is not tradition or dialectic skill that points us to this way, but the simple reflection of the religious perception. Then we may say with the Catechism, "Jesus Christ, truly God, begotten of the Father in eternity, and also truly man, born of the Virgin Mary, is my Lord." Christ is the God who makes the history of humanity a history of redemption, or makes humanity a Church; and again, He is the historical man into whom this personal will of God entered, who made it the content of His life, and has introduced it as historically operative power into the life of humanity.

Thus, then, the question which led to this

discussion is answered. It was the eternal will of God for the salvation of man which created and formed the man Jesus as its organ, and through Him realised the eternal decree that a Church should exist. This will was before the man Jesus, and it continues to exist so long as there is a history or a humanity in need of salvation. It became manifest to mankind in Christ; it was the "divinity of Christ"; and its continuance justifies us in the confession that Jesus Christ "lives and reigns to all eternity." Now, if one should ask what has become of the human soul of Jesus, or how it is constituted at present, or where it is now, we should answer, it is in God and God is in it; but with regard to the particular psychical and physical mode of existence of Jesus' humanity, we must confess that that is beyond the limits of human knowledge.

The effects produced reveal the being to us. Whether what has been said of Christ's being is tenable will show itself in the next lecture, when Christ's work will be discussed.

LECTURE XIII

THE WORK OF CHRIST

THE subject of the last lecture was Christ. The personal Divine will for the salvation of mankind became manifest and operative in the man Jesus. Jesus Christ was God and man.

Now, the further question arises, whether this result finds confirmation in the working of Jesus. It is not our intention to seek for purely theoretical thoughts such as might be of interest to the historian or the philosopher; we wish to understand Christ, as the plain Christian perceives Him on account of the loving-kindness of Christ which he has experienced. Only those thoughts of Christ are necessary which can be shown to be necessary from His work. Thus He worked; hence He must have been correspondingly constituted.

The question as to the work of Christ has all along found two answers. Christ characterised Himself as the revelation of God: "No man knoweth the Father, save the Son, and he to whomsoever the Son willeth to reveal Him." "He that hath seen Me hath seen the Father." He is the way, the truth, and the life for sinners. But the Good Shepherd gives His life too for the sheep. "I am not come to be ministered unto, but to minister, and to give My life a ransom for many." The purpose of His blood or His violent death is the forgiveness of sins. Christ reveals God to us and leads us thereby to God, and He gives His life for us and makes us thereby well-pleasing and righteous in God's sight. He works from God upon us, and He works from us upon God. Christ is the founder of the "New Covenant." That is no indefinite thought, but has, according to Jer. xxxi. 31, a double, precisely defined content: it was the programme of Jesus' working. God will write His will inwardly in men's hearts, and He will forgive them their sins. That is the "New Testament" in opposition to the Old Covenant. There God commanded through outward precepts; here He transforms the hearts inwardly according to His will and forgives sin. In the New Covenant God realises His sovereignty.

So it has remained. Both thoughts meet us constantly in the New Testament, and they have never died out in the history of Christianity. We continually hear the new lawgiver, the teacher and prophet praised who has brought us the divine life; and we hear the thankful confession that He offered Himself to God in our stead for the forgiveness of our sins.

As a rule both thoughts are combined, but it has also been possible for them to stand in relative opposition to each other, as may be seen already in the Middle Ages. Anselm conceived of Christ's work as the vicarious satisfaction which had to be offered to God as the insulted Lord, in order to secure His forgiveness for sins. But in opposition to him, Abelard taught that Christ was the revelation of God's love, which awakes responsive love in us.

Both views have remained till the present day. Theologians' criticism of the one or the other, and the various attempts to unite them, do not interest us here. Let us try to come to an understanding of the matter.

Our standpoint cannot be taken anywhere else than in the soul of the Christian of to-day. What does he experience in Christ, what does Christ become to him?

This question is for the present very easy to answer. Many voices have been heard in our soul, and they have brought forth in us much that is great and good. But one voice made the other dumb, and one authority overpowered the other, hence none could captivate our inmost heart for ever. Then a historical form arose before our soul. Simple and clear was what it bore witness of to us, and what it became to us. But it was not the clearness of the reasons, not the simplicity of the claims that captivated us. From this form there came home to our heart the power of personal life, a strong, almighty will, the holy power of love. This will laid hold on us and subdued us. It would have us, therefore we would have it. Jesus Christ became for us the absolute fixed authority which ever again drove us to the experience, "Lord, to whom shall we go? Thou hast the words of eternal life." He became our Lord, and in Him we came to know the sovereignty of God. That is what is new in Christ. There was much in His teaching that was known before. The ruling divine power of His person was the new element.

That is the experience of the divinity of Christ. He and He alone among all the figures and powers of life constrains us to faith and love. We accept what He says to us, what He gives us and what He becomes to us, and thereby we are inwardly freed to follow Him, to make His goal ours, to love God and the brethren with holy, eternal love. That He is the Lord and exercises divine sway over us we experience in faith, and that His goal, or the Kingdom of God, is the only really precious good we prove—through His power, and because He actuates us to it—in love. Jesus Christ is holy Spirit. Since He penetrates the heart and subdues us, we become free from the world and from ourselves, and it is then we feel ourselves in the sphere of life, upon the heights of our existence.

Perhaps that sounds cold and abstract, but yet it sums up in itself the whole of the marvellous riches of Jesus' will and Jesus' life. We think on His words about the Father in heaven, on the blessed freedom from care which the birds of heaven and the lilies of the field proclaim. We think on His promises of protection to believers, and of judgment which shall finally procure right for them. We call to mind His warning not to fear those who can kill the body, but have no power over the soul, and the spirit of victory in which He met death and triumphed over it. What else does all this tell us but the great truth that God is for us and therefore all things must work together for our good? That is the faith which embraces thousand circumstances and is experienced in all possible dispensations and arrangements of life's path, and which is still only the one great experience, namely, God is our God; God is for us, therefore we have peace in spite of sin and guilt; God is the power of our life, therefore we must succeed.

We realise all the glorious words, many of which were difficult before, but now have become easy: the admonition to follow Him and leave all else, to strive after the kingdom alone, to love our fellow-men, even our enemies, to give ourselves heart and soul and all we have to their service. We call to mind the exposition of the old law in the Sermon on the Mount. We remember the words about God, who makes His sun to rise upon the just and the unjust. We remember the prayer of Christ for His enemies, His humble service for sinners —who would not have a rich life to live on all that, and who would not feel how great and pure the soul becomes that really follows Christ? But what else do all these thoughts impress upon us than the simple, great truth that our life is for God, and, since for God, for the brethren also? It is love. "We love, because He first loved us. If any man say, I love God, and hateth his brother, he is a liar; for he that loveth not his brother whom he hath seen, how can he love God whom he hath not seen? And this commandment have we from Him, that he who loveth God love his brother also."

That is what Christ proclaimed: God is for us, therefore all things serve us; and we are for God, therefore we serve all. And this is the task He lays upon us, not as a law or a theoretical doctrine, but as a gift which we experience, feel, and have in the coming of God's sovereignty over us. Sovereignty and faith, Kingdom and love—that is the essence of

Christianity as Christ proclaimed it and as He has made it manifest to us, attainable, efficacious, and real.

Because He exercises God's sovereignty in our heart and thereby brings us to faith; and because He shows us the Kingdom of God and thereby leads us to love; because He produces spirituality in us and directs us to the divine, He is our Lord and we pray to Him—and we know that prayer can be made only to God—we submit our souls to Him with all the powers and gifts we have. No one would do that, and no one could acknowledge such an action if he had not experienced and felt that Christ leads him to the summit of creation, that He makes us what God intended us to be.

It is this experience that leads us to the confession of the divinity of Christ. He has worked as God, for what He has produced in us is divine.

But let us turn now to the other question, namely, the meaning of the human life of

Christ for our salvation. That leads us to the question of the forgiveness of sins. What Jeremiah says of the new covenant has to do not only with the new religious and moral life in the heart, but also with the forgiveness of sins.

There can be no religious faith which does not at the same time include the consciousness of the forgiveness of sins. We are sinners, and the higher our soul rises in the service of Christ, the clearer do we see the sin in us; the more His spirit penetrates us, the more restlessly do the impulses of sin and the lusts of the world revive in us. No one lives in communion with Christ without becoming more sensible of the number and heinousness of his sins and of the depth of his guilt than before.

But in this communion there is a wonderful element. We regularly exercise a judgment on self which we characterise as the activity of conscience. In communion with Christ we see and condemn our sins most strictly and yet at the same time we feel them forgiven. We can remain glad and blessed on the heights, if we believe in Christ, in spite of our sin and its baseness.

How is that possible ? How can He who quickens our consciousness of sin at the same time remove it ? How can He in whose light we first know sin give us the certainty of its forgiveness ?

A great paradox opens to our thought. The holy God, whom the sinner cannot perceive—for sin tears the soul away from the preception of God ; it makes godless or looses from God—wills to be the sinner's God. And the holy and sinless Christ gives us the consciousness of the forgiveness of sins and grace. And further, precisely with those things which human sin and wickedness did to Christ, the Righteous, is connected for Christendom in all ages the consciousness of forgiveness. What is absurd and contradictory cannot be believed, hence Christendom always strives to reach an explanation of this fact, and faith itself demands such an explanation. We give expression to the thoughts of faith while we seek to understand them.

If through Jesus Christ the relation between God and man has become a new one, so that we have in Him the forgiveness we did not have before, then something must have happened in the history of man through Christ which explains this change. And certainly a new element has made its appearance, a new principle has been introduced into history.

There was a man who stood in the midst of the sinful world, who felt all its allurements and temptations—for He was "in all points tempted like as we are"—who tasted all the threatenings and terrors, all the sufferings and grief, which are consequences of sin, to the uttermost, the death of the innocently condemned, the bitterness of feeling Himself forsaken of God ; and this man remained—in all that, and in spite of all that, in the "world" and in opposition to the "world"—faithful to God ; He remained the organ of the Divine will. The world spared Him nothing ; it exhausted its wickedness on Him, but He remained God's, and His love failed not.

That was not something self-evident—there had never been the like—and it was no small thing, because it happened in a far-off corner of the Roman Empire, and not in Rome; because it is not the formulæ of philosophy and the forms of earthly power that attached themselves to it, but the faith and love of simple souls. It was something vast, with which nothing, absolutely nothing, in the history of mankind can be compared. The soul of man decides over the course of history, and not philosophy or the state. What prophets had prophesied, what poets and thinkers had in imagination dreamed and demanded—and whatever had been was like a wondrous melody that came, but passed again, as if in the sighing of the wind—became reality in one human soul. It is possible to serve God in the midst of worldly affairs; it is possible to keep the soul great and pure in the midst of the pleasure and pain of mankind. In those days in Galilee and Jerusalem a new human type was created, a miracle was performed, to which no other can be even distantly compared, something became real before which all the great deeds of the mind dissolve into nothing.

The life of Jesus, and that His *human* personal life—that is the all-important point here—was this miracle and this new creation. Humanity had again become the organ of God, and precious to Him; its existence had again received a meaning in the existence of the world, and thereby it had justified its right to exist; it disturbs no more God's world-plan—that there be a good humanity that shall serve Him, and consciously further the highest end,—but applies itself to it and serves it.

But did, then, such a humanity exist? Was there not only a wonderful man, an ideal that could become real on account of the particular and unique relation of Him who held it to God, an ideal that could be attained by no other, and which precisely on that account repels and condemns the rest of mankind all the more, and shows their worthlessness and purposelessness?

This leads back to the former train of thought. This man was no far-off, lifeless ideal; He possessed the divine power of binding human hearts to Himself, and subjecting them to His mind and purpose. Kant characterised Christ as the " ideal of a humanity well-pleasing in the sight of God." That is not enough. This ideal lived, and in it was the almighty power of God. Christ changed mankind and drew them after Him, for He was able to give them faith and love.

So in Him stood the new humanity in the old world before the eyes of God and the eyes of the world, and through Him it was guaranteed that this new humanity is being realised, for He binds men to Himself and makes them followers of Him in His path.

That was God's way of redeeming man. It has now to be considered somewhat more minutely. The revelation of God shows its eternity in being power for all men, since all ages can understand it. It does not concern us whether this way of redemption was "in itself" necessary for God, but why it was necessary for man; for only thereby was it necessary for God. The way of redemption is the way of the cross of Christ. In that, all New Testament books are at one. But the cross of Christ teaches us to know the greatness of the love of God, who gives up the one Just One to death for the redemption of many. But the cross of Christ also brings home to us the holy earnestness of God, who forgives the guilt of sin only when the break with evil is made certain. The cross of Christ is the highest expression of the love of God, and the heaviest judgment on the sin of mankind. Not only the former, but also the latter had to be learned by mankind. The love of God had to be experienced together with His holy earnestness; blessedness had to be apprehended together with horror of sin. It was only so that redemption advanced beyond emotion of soul to peace of conscience; only so could the certainty of forgiveness of sins take its place in the new life; only so could redemption still the depths of moral feeling. Jesus Christ breaks the power of sin in us through the divine power of His holy Spirit, and He overcomes the consciousness of guilt in us through His holy humanity proved true on the cross. In the first He works as God upon us; in the last as man for us men upon God. There we perceive Him to be God's prophet and king, here to be our high priest.

But it is this second point that calls for attention here. A historical individual has consummated the breach with the world and sin—it is the last burden of our soul—and asserted it, bidding defiance to all pleasure and pain of the world. This man was the new humanity, the "second Adam," as Paul says. He represents in Himself—concrete and visible, sensible to hearts and calling them to follow— the new, holy humanity to man, which through the Spirit overcomes the world. But mankind saw also in His figure man as he is accepted before God. And nowhere did that come so impressively and powerfully to light as in His sufferings. Even when He felt Himself forsaken of God, He remained faithful to Him; even when the bitter cup of suffering was put into His hands, He continued faithfully in His service for the brethren. He bore sufferings for them which He had not deserved, and He did for them what they did not do. In that way He is their representative and their surety before God. The man who is accepted before God, became our brother and surety even unto death. And God recognised Him as such through the resurrection from the dead. On that account there grew out of His life and sufferings the view that He "stands in our stead" before God, and that through Him we, with our God-opposing, sinful nature, are "covered" before God, or that He is the atoner for our sin, and that God sees us as "righteous" in Him, and forgives our sin.

Is this view unwarranted? It is at once unwarranted when taken as if there were no

THE WORK OF CHRIST 255

spiritual connection between us and Christ. But this connection is present in faith, as we have seen. And again, it is unwarranted when Christ's work is looked on as if it were a human invention—magic in the sublimest sense—to "incline God in our favour." It was God Himself who sent Christ and determined Him for this work—the cup of suffering which He drank was given Him by the Father, His suffering was a necessity—and Christ works upon God so far as God lets Himself be worked upon for our salvation. Jesus Christ, in fact, atoned for our sin and represented us before God. The work of Christ may be summed up in the two conceptions of vicarious atonement and vicarious surety. The former demands His full humanity; the latter takes place through the power and certainty of His divine life. Under the oppression of all the powers of sin and suffering He remained the new, ideal man who is precious in God's sight, and who furthers God's design with all His power. Thereby He made atonement for our sin before God and our conscience. Through Him and in Him we have again become God's— His property, a people ready to serve Him. But we could never really become so unless His divine power brought us back to God and subdued us to Him. And it is precisely thereby that Christ becomes our vicarious surety. He who atones for the sin of mankind is at the same time their surety with God. And now our heart may be certain that in Christ, and in virtue of our inward connection with Him, we really have forgiveness of our sins, are graciously accepted by God, and live in a new relation of reconciliation and under a new covenant. It is henceforth no illusive representation to say, God demands thee for His property again, and He forgives thee thy sin. The historical fact of the holy obedience of Christ in the realm and world of sinners, and the fact of His power over our heart make that great offer of grace intelligible and real to us. He has upheld what is good and righteous in humanity, and draws us on to follow in His path. So we understand, and can believe with pure, clear conscience, we really become God's property again; the Holy One again accepts us; the Righteous One forgives us; for Christ atoned for our sin, and He is surety for our new life. The old has truly passed away, and all things have become new through Jesus Christ, our Lord.

Every great and good life has in its own way such a vicarious meaning, it makes atonement, and it stands surety. The influence of a man's good aim enhances the worth of his whole surrounding—of his family, his colleagues, etc. And if such a man suffers from his surrounding for following the good, the victorious power of the good that is thereby established acts as an atonement, and, like a protecting cover, covers the sin of his persecutors, for the power of the good has become manifest and been maintained in opposition to wickedness. The good has conquered, in spite of outward defeat, and it becomes the surety for the final subjection of all under its power.

Since Jesus Christ, the Righteous, endured all sufferings without wavering in His righteousness, He confirmed the power of the good and made atonement thereby, in His suffering and death, for the sin of humanity.

That is why the cross stands at the middle point of the Christian religion. On that account the tempted and the suffering, the living and the dying find their comfort above all in the suffering and death, the blood and wounds of Christ. That Jesus endured even to the cross shows that He really wills to redeem us. That on the cross He remained faithful to the Father, shows that He can redeem us. The cross is the sign of the unyielding power of the good in the most dreadful hour of wickedness and pain. It is the atonement for the sin of mankind.

To sum up, Jesus Christ subdues men's hearts to Himself in faith. He is the perfect man, who represents the race before God and makes atonement for the sin of mankind, standing as their surety with His divine power.

So Christ becomes our Lord, who subdues us to God through faith and breaks sin in us, and who, through the vision of His atoning pure humanity, assures us of real and lasting forgiveness of our sin.

Nothing can then be so absurd as the assertion that the beginning of the new life in us, the germs of our merits, is the ground of the forgiveness of sins. The ground is Christ alone, that Christ who has realised in Himself the new humanity and made us members of it through the power of His love.

I know these thoughts are different from the popular theories, but I am convinced that they lose no religious possession when compared with the current conception, where the wrath of God is represented as so strictly, and with such just exactness appeased through the vicarious suffering of Christ, through His sacrifice, that God *had* to forgive. These thoughts are liable to attack at too many points to give satisfaction. (1) God appears here to be thought of as a changeable Being who is at one time angry, at another time loves. (2) That God Himself sends Christ out of love is not clear. (3) The ancient idea of the "suffering God" plays a part, in an infinite equivalent being offered for an "infinite sin." But it is only with the greatest difficulty that this painful integral calculus can be worked out, and it does not tally for all that. The idea of the "suffering God," though profound in itself, purports that Deity so stoops to mankind as to have a fellow-feeling with suffering. But that is only a pious way of thinking, which cannot be applied strictly, because it makes God changeable and dependent on the creature. (4) The conception of sacrifice in this theory is taken from heathen religiousness; here the idea of the *deus platacus* and the power of the offering to change God's intention, are at home. But that is certainly not the biblical conception of sacrifice. (5) Finally, the whole theory oscillates between two different stages of re-

THE WORK OF CHRIST 261

ligion; at first religion is thought of as a legal relation after the manner of the morality religion (*v.* p. 15), then as a redemptive religion. A different conception of God and religion are alternately applied. But to understand the Christian religion we must start from the Christian thought of God. It, too, certainly includes the strict righteousness of God over against sin, but never on that account looks on God's relation to the world as an abstract legal relation.

Let us, however, return to the thoughts developed above. But if men will apply the idea of sacrifice to Christ—in the New Testament that is done only in one of the latest writings, the Epistle to the Hebrews, with a special apologetic aim,—the connecting link must naturally be sought in the biblical idea of sacrifice as given in the Old Testament. But Old Testament sacrifice represents, in its deepest significance, a gift from man to God, which pictures the giving up of self to God, and it is an ordinance which God Himself graciously bestows upon sinners, an ordinance not to "cover" God's wrath, as the heathen conception is, but to cover the sin of mankind. In this sense Jesus Christ is the offering of mankind which is brought to God, and which God accepts and approves for forgiveness, because He has determined it thereto. If the thought of sacrifice, in this its only possible biblical sense, be applied to the work of Christ, it corresponds fully with the view of the meaning of Christ's death, which has been developed above. So it is quite right to speak of redemption through Christ's sacrifice so long as it is clearly understood what is thereby meant. But the thoughtless and ignorant manner in which a conception of sacrifice, which quite clearly arises from the vulgar ideas which come from Paganism, is first formed and then declared the norm for the understanding of the work of Christ, must be decidedly rejected. Since such suggestions can be only too easily united with the conception of sacrifice, seeing it is no more current nowadays, it would be wise to employ it only cautiously.

The objection might be raised against our view that it, too, represents God as changeable. But the coming of Christ realises, as we understand it, an eternal decision of the Will, which, for the sake of man, entered into the reality of the world at a particular point of time, when humanity had become ripe to understand it. It is not God who is changed through Christ's atoning work, but through Christ God changes the relation that exists between Him and mankind by putting the change in forms which can be understood. To that end Christ died for us.

In conclusion it may be said that our knowledge of the person of Christ is confirmed through the consideration of His work. The effects of this work on the history of mankind and on the human soul, and how they are constituted, remain to be further investigated.

LECTURE XIV

THE CHURCH OF JESUS CHRIST

THE entrance of Jesus Christ into the history of the civilised world has divided it into two camps. "I came to cast fire upon the earth; and what will I if it is already kindled?" "I came not to send peace, but a sword." The one party is for Him, the other against Him. The one receives from Him a new, exalted existence and forgiveness of sins—the new covenant; the other throws aside the new covenant for divers reasons and unreasons.

Jesus Christ is a phenomenon in the world's history; His life is a new operative principle. The content of His life was the Divine will that a humanity arise which should serve God in faith and love. This will has been realised

THE CHURCH OF JESUS CHRIST 265

in the Christian Church. His life and His will produce the Church and give it life; He moves and upholds it. This was recognised by the Apostle Paul, and this recognition belongs to the greatest of his thoughts. There existed a number of Christian Churches, far apart from each other, without common organisation or constitution, without conscious and concerted community of aims of action. It was not temporal bands, not human strength that bound them together. They glowed like lights here and there on a broad dark landscape. But the prophetic eye of the Apostle saw in them a unity; he saw the mighty conflagration in which the old world passes away, and out of which a new world arises.

How did Paul come to this remarkable, this bold idea? It was given him through faith in Jesus Christ. He is the Lord, whose almighty love embraces the many children of men in a unity. He is the head, and the body cannot be wanting. He who fills all things wills that the Church reach a state in which His fulness will be manifest. He is the husband and the Church His wife, as of old the people Israel was looked on as Jahve's married wife.

The almighty will of Christ the Lord fulfils itself; He creates for Himself a Church which follows Him. Whether that Church be small or great, however loose the connection of its parts may be, it is guaranteed through Christ's will as the kernel of mankind, as the gold in history, as the historical organ of the operations of the Divine Spirit, and hence as the communion in which is the highest progress that the human spirit can reach.

And this community existed and grew, as the mustard seed grew into a tree; it was the net which drew many from the deep. This was the Christian Church. Had Jesus won only individual souls here and there, holy recluses and lonely spirits, His work would have been ruined and His will would have remained unfulfilled. Celsus or Voltaire must then have been right. What one man had built up with his poor followers, other men of greater genius could and must have destroyed. But out of the *écrasez l'infâme* hurled against the Church, nothing has ever come. For it was not the believers' strength of conviction, nor yet the blood of the martyrs, but the spirit of Jesus Christ that was the foundation and seed of the Christian Church.

But nothing that God wills and accomplishes in the history of mankind is unnatural or contrary to human nature, for God Himself has created that nature as the organ of His will. Though the capacities and inclinations of this nature may serve as paths for the powers of evil, they are also the ways by which the Holy Spirit moves. This holds with reference to the Church also. The will of Christ that His Church exist, needed human nature with its tendencies and inclinations as means for raising the structure. Man lives not solitarily, but socially. The greatest that he experiences, thinks, and wills, he thinks and wills for others. He speaks and acts out of and about what moves his heart. So the men who inwardly experienced the sovereignty of Christ could not act otherwise than for the advancement of this sovereignty. "We cannot but speak the things which we have seen and heard." They came with their experience to other men; they persuaded and convinced; they worked through their life and won through their death. So they carried on Christ's work in word and deed, in action and suffering. It was Christ's will that mankind become the Kingdom of God. They applied this will to individuals according to their nature and their need, expounding and bringing nearer to them the sovereignty and the Kingdom.

And this their will, these their words— one may think of the apostles, or just as well call to mind the mother who teaches her child to pray, or the friend who wishes to convince the friend—found a hearing, and went home to the heart as an expression of the almighty will of God concerning the individual soul. The soul experienced in these words the nearness

THE CHURCH OF JESUS CHRIST 269

of God, as if it heard a voice saying, I will have thee for mine. Thousands experienced the sovereignty and the Kingdom. And faith in it and love became the common possession and the common spirit of a group of men. But this common element existed for the individuals, overcame the individuals, and made them members of the whole. And precisely in this is expressed and revealed its power.

And this divine power which gives life to the Church in strengthening and uplifting through the words of its members, in awakening and stirring up, was experienced by Christendom as the Holy Spirit which Christ had promised to send to His Church. The God who wills that the individuals be His, and bends them under His sovereignty and fits them into His Kingdom, is the Holy Spirit. The Holy Spirit is the almighty power from above, which frees the soul from the earthly and the everyday, and fills it with life. In ancient Christendom the effects produced by this Spirit were felt with the force of natural effects; for example, the gift of healing or the ecstatic speaking with tongues. That has ceased. But we still experience the Spirit from above as operative spiritual will-power. There is something constraining, overpowering in the operation of the Spirit. All the light He sheds into my soul, all the conceptions He brings home to my heart, are summed up finally in the deep experience that an almighty power has come over me and claims me as its own. Christ's will that a Church exist is realised by the operativeness of the Spirit in the individuals, and, out of the fulness of the grace-bestowing will revealed to man in Christ the Spirit goes forth as eternal will-power to bring the individual soul into subjection to God.

So the Christian Church is the realisation of the will of Jesus Christ; but it becomes so because the Holy Spirit makes the God-power to operate upon its members to the intent that thou and I and many individual souls become God's. The Church is the product of Jesus Christ, and it is the product of

THE CHURCH OF JESUS CHRIST 271

the Holy Spirit, and it is so because the Holy Spirit masters the former, as a will masters the whole, only in so far as the Church wills the particular individual parts.

In this way the Christian Church arose. It may be regarded as the work of Jesus Christ, or looked on as the product of the propaganda of the religious ideas of Christendom, or judged of as the work of the Holy Spirit. But all this is only a clearer way of expressing the one thought that the Church consists of those men whom God makes subject to His sway by leading them to His Kingdom.

He who recognises this connection cannot think it strange that Jesus laid before His disciples definite forms for the furtherance of His cause in the world. They are three: the preached gospel word, and in support of it the work of love, baptism in God's name, and the repetition of the Last Supper which Jesus held with His disciples.

The effects of influence are produced through

word and sign, therefore Jesus chose these means. The word is simply *the* means of communicating spiritual meanings and emotions. So, on the choice of it, nothing more need be said. It was simply necessary. But since the word spoken concerning Jesus and His sovereignty is an expression of the divine will as to man, these human words become at the same time manifestations of the Spirit and the power of God. Nothing specially ecclesiastical in the official sense is to be thought of in regard to the word as a means of grace, nor anything solemn or abstract. Where one wishes to make another subject to the sovereignty of God, he wills it from God, and what he wills and speaks is the expression of the will of God, and his word takes effect in so far as it is heard at all, and works psychologically as almighty divine will. We all—the young too, and even the erring—speak God's word in so far as we speak of God's sovereignty, for our speech is the vehicle of the power of God.

THE CHURCH OF JESUS CHRIST 273

But how can God's word be spoken or become a historical power unless it is followed by those who speak as well as by those to whom they speak? The word is accompanied by faith and love. That the word is spirit and life is shown constantly by the fact that it does not exist or live without the gift of the spirit and of life, without faith and love. There may be exceptions here and there where the word is proclaimed without the power of faith and the exemplification of love. The life of Christendom as a whole must see to it that these exceptions are recognised as such.

What the word says often and in divers forms of expression capable of different meaning, baptism has brought us as a single act. The form of the Christian baptism is connected with the baptism of John, which in its turn went back upon the baptism of proselytes. Washings of that kind served not seldom as religious symbols in those times. Christian baptism transmits to the soul nothing else than the word of evangelic preaching brings it. In the fact that it happens only once lies its meaning for the Christian soul. Once for all it is fixed and said to the soul that it belongs to God, and that He gives it forgiveness and life. In the anxiety of misunderstanding and in the distress of misapprehension the soul can take comfort in this, that God's sovereignty over it is consummated with its gifts and its tasks. In this connection infant baptism, which has become usual in the Church, can easily be understood. It is not a question of an infusing of "germs of new life" in baptism—what could that mean?— God places the child under His sovereignty and love; the child has been brought into this sphere and is to be kept in it. That signifies not less than those "germs," but more, for it is all that God gives the soul. But just as infant baptism took its place in the Church only after the Church became the people's Church, so its continuance now presupposes the presence of a Christian communion in which the child is able gradually to appropriate to itself the gifts given it by God in baptism.

There is a very ancient liturgical word—known already by Paul, 1 Cor. xvi. 22—which expresses simply to us the religious meaning of the Last Supper. It is Marana tha, "Come, Lord." It is found in the conclusion of the old communion liturgy. It was this that the receivers of bread and wine, according to Christ's appointment, expected, namely, that Christ should be present in that hour among them with His love and His power, as once at that last supper which He held with His disciples. "Behold, I stand at the door and knock: if any man hear my voice, and open the door, I will come in to him, and will sup with him, and he with me" (Rev. iii. 20). "Having loved his own, he loved them unto the end." That was the frame of mind at that last supper in the circle of the disciples. That He is present to His disciples as on that evening in living nearness with the gifts and blessings of His new covenant is the faith which each Christian celebration of the Supper presupposes, begets, and deepens.

Since such is the state of affairs with regard to the Church and the means of its existence, it was a historical necessity that, in proportion as the Church spread in the world and the free life of the Spirit showed itself in habits and forms, care should be taken for the regular use of the means of Christian propaganda and self-preservation. From this consideration follows the necessity of the ecclesiastical office, as also the duty of this office. There is only one office necessary in the Church—that is the preacher's office—and it is therefore the "highest office" in the Church, as the Augsburg Confession says. Its sole duty and aim is to proclaim Christ, and thereby and only thereby to subject souls to the sovereignty of God. The realisation of God's government is the deepest ground and reason of ecclesiastical rule.

That happens especially through preaching, and by this duty its nature must be determined

THE CHURCH OF JESUS CHRIST 277

in the various ages of history according to the needs of the congregation. If preaching is to be efficacious, the ecclesiastical office will also have to exercise an educational activity on the congregation. The instruction of the young and the care for souls are just as important here as the guidance to the works of the Home Mission or the ecclesiastical arrangements for co-operation in the solution of the great religious and moral problems of the day, such as the social question at present. It is only a sign of natural development that in recent times Christendom's manifold labour of love is advanced quite specially by free societies and not solely by the organised Church.

So the work of the Church develops to a widely extending activity that enters into the most manifold provinces of life. In this lies the ground of the Church's entering as a whole into a permanent historical connection with the surrounding world. It experiences a history so far as it takes part in the collective life-and-culture-movement of mankind.

The Church must not be separated from the total mental movement of history. The measure of its effects can hardly be taken broad and great enough. It is an external and lower conception when the word "Church" is used for Churches and ministers, for particular ritual acts or for the visible organism. The Church advances God's cause in the world, and therefore also the interests of human souls; it is the chief educator of the human spirit. The Church is the protector of the greatest goods and most precious possessions of history, and the stream of life which gives power to the fields of humanity to bring forth, instead of the reeds and flowers of pseudo-culture, the strong bread-fruit which is necessary for the real progress of the mind.

The recognition that Christianity is the absolute religion determines the recognition of the significance of the Church. While all other religious societies and all schools and tendencies relapse into the world and the spirit and life in them is gradually destroyed

THE CHURCH OF JESUS CHRIST 279

and broken by the world, there lives and reigns in the Church the Holy Spirit and eternal life. From the Church holy life can always stream anew into the dying world, and from it the sovereignty of God intervenes ever anew in the history of the human spirit. It is no high-flown, romantic fancy, but the expression of the simple thought that Jesus' words and Jesus' spirit live and are borne witness to in Christendom, and that therefore the power of God becomes manifest in it. But that means it is the proclamation of the Church that raises man to the highest point of his nature. This should now be clear.

So the human race needs the Church as the historical source of eternal life. Such statements are often looked on as a mere glorification of the Church, and offence is taken at them on that account. But it must not be overlooked how infinitely difficult and responsible duties arise therefrom for the Church.

But if this is so, then the Church has a

fixed and necessary relation to the world and its history. Missionary and apologetic work, the criticism of the world's condition and the preaching of eternal life are not subjective whims of people who have nothing else to do, nor "pious obtrusiveness"—as is probably often thought—but represent the fulfilment of the Church's tasks in the history of the world. So long as the Church exists they are there, and so long as they are there the Church continues to exist.

Where this is understood, it will also be agreed that precisely because the Church stands in a fixed relation of infinite importance to the world it must never become secularised. For only if the spirit of Christ alone reign in it, if it holds itself inwardly free from the world, can it give its service to the world. A secular Church is of no use to the world; a spiritual Church means everything for the world. In other words, the Church shall be free. It is free if Jesus Christ is its Lord, He alone.

But it is precisely on account of this inner freedom from the world that the Church is capable of entering into the closest and conscious relation to the world. This relation is its task.

This relation demands first that the ecclesiastical world of thought should assert itself over against the view of the world held by the particular age and should receive the forms which make it capable of doing so. Therewith the task of theological science and its connection with the world's scientific movement is characterised. The Church needs theology to enable it to carry on its work. But, on the other hand, it is involved in this relation that conflicts between Church and theology can from the nature of the case scarcely be avoided. The leaders in the life of the Church hold, as a rule, that the forms and ideas in which they grew up and with which they worked are the best, or even the only possible ones, and so raise objection or else remain indifferent to the results of the progress of scientific knowledge, and that all the more as the representatives of science, on the other hand, have also a tendency to set up their latest knowledge and observations prematurely as the truth to which the future belongs, and to oppose the common and usual as foolish and detrimental. From this there arises a conflict of minds in which old and new struggle with each other with changing fortune according to the side on which the power of truth or the opportuneness of the situation is greater. But faith is certain that truth will win the victory.

From the connection with the world must result a second movement. The Church enters into a relation with the State. The State looks on the Church as a legal institution, which means that the Church must adhere to a fixed doctrine, organisation, and constitution. The State will always make this legal demand of religious denominations and grant protection to Churches on the ground of its fulfilment, just as any "recognised" society enjoys the privilege of legal pro-

THE CHURCH OF JESUS CHRIST 283

tection in so far as it conforms to its statutes and the activity organised by them. The question is whether the State contents itself with this part or claims an administrative direction of the life of the Church. The former is the case with the Free Churches; the latter is the historical form of Protestantism in Germany. The princes take the place of superior bishops, and Church courts are appointed by them to govern the Church. Thus the Church government in our Churches is an ecclesiastical court appointed by the State to guide the administration of the Church, and to attend to the preservation and carrying out of canon law and Church constitution. From this it is clear how endlessly difficult, complicated, and contradictory the position of Church government in the majority of the Protestant Churches is. On the one side, the life of the Church is to be guided according to established laws; on the other, one cannot avoid seeing that these laws are not always adequate and applicable. On the one hand, judgment must be passed in accordance with the spiritual norms of the Church; on the other, the temporal interests of the State are the standard.

But all these forms belong to history and are thereby more than mere outward forms; they penetrate deep into the life of the Church. Therein lies their importance, but also their danger. They maintain the historical continuity of development over against the inconstant vagaries of new notions and fashionable tendencies. But they are also always exposed to the bureaucratic danger of "quenching the Spirit" and setting up compromises to the truth. When it is understood how all the power of the Church lies in its spiritual freedom over against the world, this danger will not be depreciated, and it will at least be understood when one of our most brilliant jurists closes a recent work on "Church Law" with the sentence, "The nature of Church law stands in contradiction to the nature of the

THE CHURCH OF JESUS CHRIST 285

Church." What is especially necessary in this matter is to take a sober view of things. Not Divine wisdom, but the administration of the law is to be expected from Church government. And its representatives are to be recognised as officials, but not in romantic, mystical phraseology to be advanced to " chief shepherds," etc. The means afforded by the Church constitution are to be diligently used, but with no other aim than the inward one of the Kingdom of God and the honour of God. It is really only another legal overestimation of Church law, when, like the abovementioned jurist, people make the Church law responsible for all the evils in the Church. Yet the difficulties to be met with represent in the long run only one side of the difficulty presented by the presence of God's Spirit in this world, and the realisation of eternal possessions in time.

But these circumstances account for the constant discontent with the Church government which accompanies Protestantism. The decisions are looked on as either too spiritual or too temporal, too narrow or too broad, not sufficiently wise or too diplomatic. It is childish or ill-minded to lay the blame on the persons. It lies in the matter itself. On the other hand, if deliverance is looked for from the "Free Church," it seems doubtless that the development of Protestantism is moving gradually towards it; for what other are the manifold and vigorous unions and societies of the Foreign and Home Mission than the beginnings of the Free Church? But nothing would be so fatal as a premature anticipation of history, as the leap in the dark which the giving up of the existing forms of the Church would mean for us.

But, to conclude, it is sufficient if an insight has been obtained into the difficulties in this province, in which we may experience something of the evolution of history.

Still one point requires to be mentioned, namely, the weal or woe of the Church may be looked on as dependent on the Church constitution or the theological work. Certainly the importance of these is great; but it is not ecclesiastical councillors and professors of theology that build the Church, but the truth of Jesus Christ, which makes Christianity operative in the heart. Here theology and Church government serve only as assistants. They exist for the sake of the ministry and serve it. But this office, too, is only a historical form conditioned by time. What it amounts to in the long run is that there are enthusiastic hearts to communicate Jesus' message. It depends on the living persons to whom religion is all, and who on that account can look beyond everything—parties and schools, Church constitution and outward successes, with their honours. " They saw Jesus only"—these are the real builders of the Church. When such persons go and come, the cause of Jesus Christ is forwarded in the world. What hinders Christ's message is therefore to be combated, and that with all one's strength. As for the rest, the ideal of the Church must be striven after, however far we still are from it.

Through the Church of Jesus Christ the sovereignty of God is extended among mankind. Human souls are directly subjected to it in eternal service. But the Church exercises, too, an immeasurable indirect influence. Who could sum up shortly what a meaning Christianity has had in the course of history for the morals and right, the science and art, the views of the world and the feelings of mankind? Even the most energetic opposers of Christianity in our midst bear somehow or other the marks of Christ in them. Even the most sober work of man follows somehow or other impulses which Jesus introduced.

So the work of the Church serves to extend the sovereignty of God. What the sovereignty of God brings to the individual souls will be the subject of the next lecture.

LECTURE XV

THE ORIGIN AND DEVELOPMENT OF THE NEW LIFE OF THE CHRISTIAN

WHAT remains still to be discussed?

Many questions present themselves at this point, an answer to which is necessary in order even approximately to exhaust our subject. These cannot be discussed now. One point, however, is so important that it must not be omitted.

Christianity has been recognised as the absolute religion. The new condition of the soul which it brings has also been discussed in that connection; then the means by which God has made Christianity a historically operative power, and the ways in which it shows itself operative in the history of mankind. At the end we see ourselves pointed again to the soul and the real life which it leads.

If we could lay hold of the new life by a simple resolution and then in its power continue in it, how blessed and joyous the days of our life would pass! But as we win all that is great and good in life gradually through laborious development and hold it through many struggles, so it is with Christianity.

This development and these struggles are the subject of the present lecture; the concluding one will treat of the goal of the development.

Personal Christianity consists in faith and love; in nothing less and in nothing more. What that means and includes in itself has been already recognised.

Everything in our soul has a beginning; so our Christianity has had a beginning. How was it effected? The answer was given in the last lecture. Heaven is not rent asunder, nor does a supernatural nature stream as by holy magic into our nature. The deeds and words through which God became manifest to the world in Jesus Christ have entered into history and live on in the Church. And these deeds and words prove their divinity in influencing us still to-day as eternal will-power. Christianity comes to us through the word, which teaches God's sovereignty and His Kingdom. This word influences us as a divine power. We experience the sovereignty of God, which persuades and overcomes us. Thereby our soul receives a new content. It experiences the operation of God, who gives it faith and love and assures it of the forgiveness of sins. This content which has been won—not the natural capacity which we call talent—makes the soul what it is. A new content means a new soul. Since God gives faith and love, He has created us anew to be a new creature; we are *born again* of God, to use the biblical expression. "Old things are passed away; behold, all things are become new."

But nothing happens in the soul that is not through the soul. That is after all the meaning of human freedom. Only that which the soul wills as its own end belongs wholly to it. The filling with new content takes place, therefore, only in so far as we comprehend this new content and consent to it in thought, will, and feeling. That is *conversion*. Thus the new birth and conversion designate the same occurrence. When it is thought of as effected by God it is called the new birth; when looked on as becoming our own through our receptive or actual activity, conversion. *The new birth is conversion.* We make use of these biblical expressions because they are known and easily understood; the expressions in themselves are of no importance. But I hope that the meaning and the inward psychological necessity of the inward occurrences designated by them are now intelligible.

That is the beginning of the Christian life. These are the first emotions of the soul in which we experience God's sovereignty and will His kingdom; that is faith and love. We feel ourselves apprehended of God, and we apprehend Him. The greater the change in the soul, the stronger the stirrings of feeling. Mighty and strong, soft and tender they thrill our heart. Great plans struggle to the surface. We feel ourselves satisfied and blessed, and we wish to be good and strong. Our aspiration is great, and the world appears small, and it seems to us simple to conquer it for our ends.

But the world is great and the relations which bind us to it endlessly complicated, and the heart is many-sided and thereby often weak and fickle. The enthusiasm of the beginning does not last. The tasks of the day demand the whole soul with all its powers, and the habits of life bring us impulses and ends which seem to have nothing in common with God's sovereignty.

And then the soul sees with terror and amazement that things are quite different from what it thought; it wishes to have faith and to love, but no occasion presents itself thereto. The remembrance is beautiful; but the present has nothing in common with it. One fares like the traveller who wanders on, map in hand. The decisive parting of the ways is marked on the map; but always new cross-roads appear of which the map says nothing.

But we wish to come to the goal. The goal was too beautiful and the impression it made too powerful to permit of our neglecting it. The goal was given us when we did not know it nor will it; *now* we *will* to hold it, but the gift threatens to disappear. The question is this, How are we to bring faith and love out of the great moments of life into the small; how is the momentary exaltation to become a *lasting* possession of the soul?

This can be done manifestly only through the means which faith and love have brought us, namely, the word. We begin to seek the word as it once sought us. We seek the Church and listen to what is said about God; we seek intercourse with Christian personalities; we seek for books which can deepen and enrich our understanding and experience of Christianity.

He that seeketh findeth. Seeking renders capable of finding in the inward life, for seeking means applying oneself to the things which one wishes. So we get answers to our questions, since the question makes the soul capable of receiving an answer. And how mightily is our soul's circle of interest now deepened and extended! The seeking already makes our soul richer. Old books and hymns which we once despised as "trash"; the religious life-experiences of others which we once good-naturedly smiled at, we begin now to understand and love. A new world of light shines in all that, and something like a new sense arises in us for the understanding of it. In this way the seeking and questioning soul experiences a development. According as it opens itself to those things, do they win entrance into it, and in the measure that they penetrate it, does the entrance for them become wider. He who will experience Christianity must not wait for it; he must seek it. And he can seek it, after the beginning has come to him. But more, he must seek it so far as this beginning urges him thereto. He to whom faith and love have come cannot do otherwise than strive after them to have them.

But it was not men but God who gave faith and love. It is God, therefore, who can preserve them to us and wills to do so. It is from God the soul expects this, and it is to God it directs itself in its seeking and questioning. That is *prayer*.

The Christian prays "in the name of Jesus." The authority of Jesus moves him to prayer. In the sphere of communion with Jesus Christ he can pray and he wills to pray, and through Jesus his prayer seems certain of being heard. That is praying in Jesus' name. It is not an arbitrary Church dogma that is designated thereby; it is not chance that so many Church prayers close with the words, "through Jesus Christ our Lord." Through Christ's life becoming the content of our soul the great came into our life. Only in communion with Christ, only through Him can we expect that

GROWTH OF THE CHRISTIAN'S NEW LIFE 297

what we received will be preserved and shielded to us. Therefore Christian prayer is " prayer in Jesus' name."

Three things are comprised in this. In the first place, the object of prayer is determined. I pray for what communion with Jesus brings me. It brings me faith and love. That is really the chief object of prayer. For this we pray categorically, in the certainty that God always wills to give us it; for it is His nature to rule, but that means to work faith and love. That is His sovereignty.

For the outward things of life we pray hypothetically, because we cannot penetrate the connection which the outward things have with the salvation of our soul. Whether expressed or not, we make such things subject to the condition, " Not my will, but Thine be done." But that means, in other words, if it inwardly furthers and exalts me, give it me; but if not, withhold it. That is the prayer of faith in Jesus' name. At the present day prayer is recommended for the purpose of healing the sick. This is in itself nothing new. The unbelieving have at all times wished to prescribe to God what He has to do and give. But this categorical asking for wonders and healings of the sick, or for money and property, however much it may be praised as "believing," is at bottom only an expression of unbelief. Faith wills to accept what God gives and works; unbelief wills that God work what we will. The unbelief that deports itself as real faith is superstition. Superstition lies finally at the bottom of all prayers of that kind.

Prayer in the name of Jesus renders intelligible to us, secondly, that we should pray together and pray for each other. Christ worked for His Church; so he who lives in communion with Him prays for the Church of Jesus Christ and for all the individuals that belong or should belong to it. Here, too, faith and love are the real object of his prayer.

Thirdly, prayer in Jesus' name assures us that our prayer is heard. Christ wills that faith and love exist, and Christ is almighty.

Therefore, he who asks for this receives it. The ways in which it comes to him are diverse. They are not always those our phantasy pictured to itself; but the goal that we willed becomes ours, so far as we pray for "the one thing needful." We prayed that suffering might be taken from us, or an outward possession given us; the former should increase our faith, the latter our love. But the suffering becomes heavier and the good removes further off, and yet we recognise with thankful heart that what we really wished has become ours, for faith and love have become stronger in the soul. In those days when outward miracles were an everyday occurrence, a great and mighty man, who has advanced the Kingdom of God more than any other, prayed that a grievous bodily malady, which hindered him in his calling as apostle, might be taken from him. He continued to pray for it, but the malady remained; and yet he knew that his prayer was heard, for the experience came to him, "My grace is sufficient for thee, for my strength is made perfect in weakness." In this he learned the lesson, "When I am weak, then am I strong." That was the Apostle Paul. This story shows us briefly how matters stand for the Christian as to the hearing of prayer. Prayer is always heard and always answered, even though our wishes and the pictures of our fancy remain unfulfilled. That points us to the barrier of faith and humility which the Christian ever erects around his prayer; he does that, not in a calculating, unwilling frame of mind, but easily and as a matter of course, for he prays in faith and in Christ's name.

That is the state of matters as regards prayer. It is a seeking and a finding. And the seeking strengthens and extends faith and love, as well as the finding.

Such is a short review of the Christian's inward development. He who goes this way has his soul filled through and through with faith and love. What does that mean? It cannot mean that every moment of his existence is filled with acts of faith and love. That is simply psychologically impossible, and it is always thoughtless to demand the impossible. Every real work and every natural occupation demands our whole undivided attention and devotion. He who fails in these, works negligently and badly. No Christian should work so. The answer to our question is different. The longer and more energetically I have taken pains with faith and love, and the more frequently I have striven after acts of faith and love, the more do faith and love become a possession and habit of my soul. They are there even when I do not perceive them, for any moment can set them free in me.

And that really happens, and in its happening there comes to us what we sought in the beginnings of our development, and what we always continue to seek. Not like an unusual guest, not like "The Maiden from afar,"[1] are faith and love henceforth to us. We have

[1] "Das Mädchen aus der Ferne," poem by Schiller.

them as the abiding, permanent possession of our soul. When we gaze upon the glory of nature, and when we feel the gifts of history; when sorrow knocks at the door of our soul like a stern warner, and when joy comes to us as a long-expected friend; when day sinks into night, and when morning greets us; when the evening song of life sounds warning in the soul, and when life's noonday calls us to action; when the great comes softly, and the small enforces its noisy claims; when gifts absorb us deeply, and tasks press upon us with loud, shrill call; when we rise to the heights, and when we are in the depths, then we have the blessed and wondrous experience of the nearness of the all-ruling God, who loves us and exalts our soul to Himself; then we feel the impulse to holy, eternal action in us, we have faith and we love. God reigns in all; Christ is the Lord of the world's history; Holy Spirit penetrates the changing correlations of life in word and deed, and the fragments of good in us are fitted into the temple of the Kingdom of God; the beginnings reach on to the goal; the manifold becomes one in the great goal; restlessness and anxiety give place to certainty and joy. "If God be for us, who, or what, can be against us?" And from the change of varying experience, from the rapture of success and the pain of disappointment, from the suffering of the world which grinds us down, and the joy in God who saves us, there arises with rejoicing the confession of our inmost soul:

> "Thee will I love, O fairest light,
> Till life's day close."

That is the development of the Christian, his self-unfolding. It realises itself in our working, but it is God's work. We sought; He causes us to find. As conversion is new birth, so is *religious self-unfolding God's preservation* in faith and love.

But one thing brings us to a dead-lock. It is sin. A new habit of life arises in us, but an old continues to exist. We will faith and love and we do not will them; for we will the world with its pleasure and its unbelief. We will both and we do not will either. That is the great conflict in our soul. The black and the white horse pull it; it is dragged left and right. It is not the butterfly that soars aloft with glittering wings, but the caterpillar in which the impulse to wing-power stirs, and yet it cannot fly.

What does that mean, and whence comes it?

It means that in our soul the wicked lust of the world and the worldly mind that overturns everything and destroys the soul are always coming into power again. This is so because the long habit of evil still determines our life.

In many ways this foreign and yet natural power makes itself felt in us. The old tendency may assert itself suddenly and contest our whole Christianity; faith is imagination, and love extravagance. Or, again, faith and love may remain in power, only there are definite points of life which are not to be touched by them. These are the favourite inclinations of man, the sweetest sins that his life knows. He wishes to be pious and earnest, if his pleasure may remain indulged in these still corners.

With strong and energetic natures the whole is questioned. The strife is short but violent; it is either—or, "all or nothing." With the softer and quieter souls, Christianity is to remain and sin to yield. But definite sins— vanity, sensuous pleasure, untruthfulness—are to be consciously kept, even if only to a definite point of time. But the latter, as the former, delays the development of the Christian. To delay the development of a thing means to repress the thing itself. The tendency of the new life is broken and the power of the good snapped. That Christianity so often passes through a sickness in the soul finds its ground in these spared and cherished sins.

What sorrier form is there than such a half Christian? He cannot enjoy the world, and he is not able to enjoy God. His faith keeps him from the one, and his sin from the other.

So he vacillates about, a walking corpse in the inward man, uncertain, rent asunder, and broken.

There are in history tensions over against which bloody struggle is relief. There are also such circumstances in personal life. This rent condition of the soul can be put a stop to only through struggle. This struggle will form the subject of the first part of the next lecture.

LECTURE XVI

THE MORAL STRUGGLE FOR THE NEW LIFE
AND ITS GOAL

WHAT is great in the different spheres of life is remarkably different and remarkably alike. The gifts are different, but the tasks they set the soul are alike as regards the faithfulness and energy, the completeness and constancy they demand. That holds of Christianity as it does of science and of the various kinds of life-work. No one can preserve the new content of the soul which Christianity brings without the application of the highest spiritual energy and faithfulness, which holds fast to what is given.

This observation, to which we were led in the last lecture, is to be applied to the moral struggle in self-maintenance also. As progress in science or art is impossible without struggle and rejection of the contradicting and limiting, so also in religion.

The new direction of faith and love is opposed, as we saw, by the old moral tendency of man. Either it turns against the whole as a whole, or one part struggles against the other; but in the latter case also the whole is at stake.

There is nothing strange or unthinkable in regard to this antithesis; it is necessary in view of the constitution of man. If the opposing elements which encounter one another in the soul of the Christian be considered and their force estimated, the terrible convulsion into which the soul falls will be understood. With all its fibres it hangs on the world, and yet it is now bound to God. Then the fibres snap; but the band too threatens to tear. The former grow quickly again. Can the latter also be again replaced? Only he becomes master of the convulsion who gains a firm point from which strength and rest go forth. Diversions cannot help us over the convulsions of life; no more do all kinds of excitements of fancy or outward penances serve the religiously convulsed soul.

On that account marvellous means of help should not be expected in this struggle. Angels do not descend from heaven to help us in it, nor does hell open to warn us; we do not receive new revelations, nor do new powers stream through us. All that would only convulse us more. We have the gospel of God's sovereignty, and we have faith and love. These are the simple and sure means by which the inner conflicts are to be overcome, and by which they can be overcome.

How simple, great, and clear are the thoughts on the revelation of God, and the spiritual contents which they give the soul as faith and love! Here lies the firm point, and here is given the inward concentration by which the soul overcomes all convulsions, perplexities, and errors. There are various turns of expression which historical tradition and ecclesiastical custom use for all this; they cause the historian much trouble in his investigations. But to the seeking soul they are collected into a simple, great revelation of God's all-operative love, and into unified experiences of the loving working of God. To impress this upon you has been one of my chief cares, for it was not of theology but of religion that I wished to speak to you. It is certainly historical soul-contents that religion brings us. But the religious understanding of these contents does not run its course in critical distinctions and logical differentiations, but in the experiencing of the whole, "of the Spirit and of power." That is not "unhistorical," for it is this whole that has changed the world's history. History, too, like dogmatics, may become a hindrance to faith, namely, if it tries to introduce in any way, no matter whether "critically" or "uncritically," the multitude of details, of differences and gradations in which it is

naturally interested into faith. Whether with
Jesus we define the divine revelation as the
sovereignty of God, or with Paul speak of
the gracious justification of the sinner, or with
John think of the eternal love and truth of
God which have been made manifest, makes
no difference here. For the practical need
of the soul it is immaterial, for all these
formulæ mediate the same to it, namely, the
experience of the almighty love of the all-
operative God, which receives the sinner and
gives him what he needs, forgiveness of
sins and a new soul, faith and love. That is
the concentration which the wrestling soul
attains to, and from which it comes to
clearness and victory in the struggle we
speak of.

A watchful, sober, simple, and observant
life is the first requirement in this struggle.
"Watch and pray," says Christ, "that ye
enter not into temptation." This must be
worked out a little in detail.

When the new inward world which the

Christian has acquired is assailed by temptation, its worth is always depreciated in his eyes. It appears of inferior value and empty compared with the goods and the pleasure which the old world offers. Impetuous, burning impulses rush through the mind in conflict with one another; so life must be conscious and watchful. We have experienced the exaltation which faith and love mean for the soul. The forgiveness and peace which faith has brought us are just as present to us as the inward health produced by the active energy of love. But while this is being experienced, another fact becomes at the same time clear, namely, the transience of worldly pleasure and the degradation and limitation which it brings into our inward life.

One must hold fast to these impressions and always picture them to oneself afresh; the various experiences which the days and weeks bring us confirm them. For this one thing is above all necessary—the soul must be cared for and time taken for its needs. He who staggers from impression to impression; he who will not wake from dreaming can win no strong, self-confident soul either in religion or in any other sphere.

This includes three elements: (1) It is not enough merely to talk of faith and love; one must really have them, one must experience them and strive after this experience; and to him who attends to this, it will be matter of amazement how faith and love come more frequently to him and in ever greater power. Faith and love will become his joy and his longing, for they revive and exalt the soul.

(2) When the allurements of the sensuous and external world threaten to darken our soul, their transience and vanity should be clearly called to mind. Savonarola kept an ivory skull on the table before him; our forefathers had Dances of Death; and we have perhaps texts hung on the wall. One gets accustomed, however, both to the bones of the dead and to texts about the vanity of this world; but life remains ever new. This life is a

great sermon on the transience of the world and the vanity of its pleasure. Let us not interrupt this sermon, but listen to the knell which accompanies our life and is heard more frequently from year to year. Nor let us fail to hear the cry or the sigh of misery that is heard behind the pleasure.

(3) And, lastly, let us strive to become masters of ourselves. The struggle in which we are involved demands it. It is a struggle with regard to another world, while we live and work in this world; and it is, finally, a struggle with regard to ourselves and the best in us. The waves of this struggle roll constantly over us. It cannot be otherwise so long as we are in this world and also of this world. It cannot be otherwise, and it must not be otherwise. So long as we wrestle inwardly we live, and the best lives in us, and we live to it. But humours and moods, idleness and the hurry of business, wrest from us ever afresh the sceptre over ourselves. For all an order of life is necessary in correspondence with their inward

spiritual need. As our calling regulates the division of our time during the day, so we should learn also to order our life from and for the highest point of view possible. No one can make such an order for another, for its power rests on individual peculiarity and adaptedness. There is so much in life that does not belong to life and yet fills up our life; it fills it up but makes it poorer; it becomes too great for us and we become thereby small. Fasting must be learned. One can fast from music and literature, from society and pleasure, just as from food. The unnecessary and inane should be avoided in life. Life must not be spent "as a tale"; it is sometimes — still worse — only a tale! That is renunciation and temperance. But in order really to serve God there must also be active discipline in service. Man should so arrange and order his life that it may become a school of discipline to him and steel him with power and self-mastery. Only he who endeavours to attain to self-mastery can serve God.

Dietetics and gymnastics must be allowed to rule in the life of the soul also. What makes us inert to faith and love should be avoided, and we should look to it that our organs are powerful and strong to serve God and His Kingdom.

We have recognised what we understand by the conscious and watchful life of the soul. The task is now to describe the moral struggle itself.

Luther's first thesis runs: " When our Lord and Master Jesus Christ says 'repent,' He means that the whole life of believers should be a repentance." Repentance is the struggle of which we speak.

What do we understand by repentance?[1] The chief element in it, according to the view of the Middle Ages, is penitence[2] or contrition. The Reformation teaches that repentance is penitence and faith. The former makes contrition the chief element, the latter conceives it as a stage on the road to faith.

[1] Busse.   [2] Reue.

THE NEW LIFE AND ITS GOAL 317

Penitence is a state of feeling in us. A particular act, or our whole moral life becomes —in so far as we are Christians—an occasion to a state of disinclination in us. Shame and disgust, pain and fear seize us, when we think of ourselves. This condition is caused by purely spiritual occurrences in us, namely, by our conscience or the moral self-judgment which we exercise in accordance with the standard of what we ourselves hold to be good. The judgment of self by the conscience produces the deep feeling of unworthiness and shame in us.

This feeling is of the greatest significance. It stirs up in us disgust and abhorrence, fear and aversion from sin. It maintains the moral capacity and disposition in us. But alone it is not enough, for the state of disinclination becomes always a motive to a positive pleasurable state; it points beyond itself and cries for compensation. Where there is nothing more than mere penitence, it will be experienced that it is presently crowded out by a new positive pleasurable feeling. The state of disinclination in penitence becomes a channel to a new sinful desire. Everyone will corroborate this observation from personal experience.

But from the Protestant point of view penitence should lead to faith, and through it to love. That is a possible demand, for penitence proceeds from faith. These acts of moral self-judgment which we characterise as conscience have for the Christian, faith and love as their standard, and they ensue from our not having had faith and love in the given case. Conscience condemns us from the standpoint of faith and love because we have not approved faith and love. Remorse or penitence thus presupposes faith and love and impels to faith and love. The sin we have committed cries for forgiveness; faith has forgiveness. And the sin under the dominion of which we fell demands for its extirpation and forgiveness, not only pain on account of it, but the power and operativeness of the new life; but that is faith and love.

That is the moral struggle in its inmost core. The Christian should give place to penitence, but he should also let it impel him forward to faith and love. They give satisfaction, whereas penitence gives only a state of disinclination. So the bad in us becomes an inward pain and torment, and this pain becomes the channel for the satisfaction of the soul through faith and love. It is only through asserting himself in spite of sin that the Christian can become master of sin. Sin is forgiven in so far as he believes in God's grace, and gives place to good in so far as he receives in faith and love the positive impulses to love. The universal victory over sin is faith and love. But the way to this height leads through the valley of penitence. Penitence is the boldest and most marvellous bridge, the bridge from death to life, from impotence to power.

That is *evangelical repentance*. The word sounds sad and dreary, like a Puritan Sunday, and it really brings only unfruitful self-torment

—unfruitful, because without positive aim—so long as penitence only is thought of. It is a psychologically impossible condition that the state of disinclination arising from penitence should for long fill the soul. It is vain to struggle for the impossible, and so the struggle is soon given up, as everyone knows. Someone does something wrong and vows "eternal penitence," but time overcomes but too soon this eternal penitence, for the purpose of it is forgotten. It is only the tendency of its own nature that the soul is following, when it lets itself be impelled through penitence to faith. Faith overcomes sin, or it leads through penitence to victory. He who repents should do it so as to strive through penitence towards faith and love.

And so it is intelligible that repentance is to the Christian a blessed word, for it is the sanctifying of his soul and it is the means by which to remain victorious in the struggle: it leads us down, but it leads us through the valley up again to the heights of the soul.

Thus the Christian fights the moral fight: it is the struggle of self-maintenance and nothing else. Man does it, and the all-operative God does it. Just as at the beginning the new birth is at the same time conversion, as the divine preservation of the new life is at the same time its personal development, so repentance or the struggle of the morally aspiring man is at the same time the sanctification which God works in his soul.

Thus the Christian goes through a religious and moral evolution. No evolution is purposeless, otherwise it would not be evolution. That brings us to the last point of which we wish to speak, namely, the goal of the religious-moral evolution. This goal is *the life-ideal, or Christian perfection.*

There is an ideal and a condition of personal perfection towards which we strive. It cannot be a question of sinlessness, or of completion, as a statue is complete, so that any further touch of the chisel only destroys. It must be something different. The Apostle Paul said once in reference to his life, "Let us, as many as be perfect, be thus minded." Before goes the confession, "I forget the things which are behind, and stretch forward to the things which are before." That is, then, Christian perfection: it is the whole-hearted coming; it is the constancy and power of aspiration out of the world to God, out of worldly pleasure and unbelief to faith and love. That this life is effected and preserved in us through Christ's redemption needs not to be repeated, for it is implied in our characterising it as faith and love.

The ideal of the Christian life is therewith characterised: towards it we should strive. It is a goal that is not in the Beyond, but can be understood and attained here on earth. To receive God's sovereignty in faith, and to realise His Kingdom in love, in constant readiness and in constant striving, receiving and giving, willing and doing, directly and in great things, indirectly and in little things, so that, thus, through this striving, the funda-

THE NEW LIFE AND ITS GOAL 323

mental intention and the fundamental direction of our life is characterised—that is the perfection of the Christian. But we live in a system full of relations to the earthly life, placed there by God, and it is only in these relations that we can experience God and serve God, for they are the framework of our life. These relations are embraced in the conception of the moral vocation, for our vocation is the expression for the God-ordered relations of our life and striving to the visible world. Hence it follows that the Christian, just because he has faith, and therefore regards his natural position in the world also as given and effected by God, must experience, exemplify, and approve his faith and his love according to the nature of his vocation. In these relations he experiences God, and in them he serves Him. They are windows to Him through which the sun shines, and organs by means of which the heart makes its thoughts operative.

One who, in his sphere of life, with its manifold relations, experiences the all-operative God and serves His Kingdom, and who wills and seeks this constantly and with all his strength, is perfect in this seeking and striving. He realises the ideal of the Christian life.

One who knows what he wills and wills what he knows is a moral character. The ideal of his life is his firm possession, and he himself has become a conscious organ of this ideal. One who consciously experiences and wills to experience the sovereignty of God, and who consciously subjects and wills to subject himself to it in faith and love is a Christian character. The Christian character is the Christian life-ideal. The Christian character is the highest form of a moral personality.

He who has reached this ideal in any measure has gained the exaltation of soul which we have found in faith and love. But this exaltation of soul is accompanied by the feeling of full satisfaction: life in faith and love is a blessed life. Blessedness is the produce of the Christian life.

But it must not be forgotten that the

THE NEW LIFE AND ITS GOAL

condition just described is not meant as a satiety or ease of the soul, as a cessation of aspiring and struggling, as a purely routine existence. Piety does not admit *pinguis Minerva*, nor does the soul live on the interest of its past—for example, with an argumentation like the well-known, " We have Abraham to our Father." This condition is, and remains, real life. Life is movement, and this life is struggle. Ever anew does the soul sink back into the dust and to the *débris* of worldly pleasure, to which it clings and adheres with the cement of self-deception; and ever anew does the almighty power of love snatch it forth to the whole, to exalted eternal life; and ever anew does this life lay hold on it with fear and pleasure. But yet the upward tendency becomes stronger and stronger; the way leads, in spite of all things, heavenward. And herein lies the "eternal youth" of the Christian soul, of which Schleiermacher speaks. To the old, in what is called "the wisdom of years," the contrasts gradually disappear;

everything becomes more and more relative and like. The Christian cannot grow old, for deep in his heart he experiences, and the longer the more vividly, the vast, bridgeless contrast between the world and God, between evil and good, between time and eternity. And from the vividness of this experience well forth, in all the freshness of youth and strength of life, pain and pleasure to the last. But pain and pleasure are the power and prerogative of youth. And in this youthful experience the consciousness of eternity that is formed in communion with the eternal God becomes personal, immediate, and fresh in the soul, even when time threatens to become master over this life.

That is it. Upon the life's path of the Christian shines the glory of eternal life, and his eye sees it, although his feet walk in the dust. The life from God is "æterna beatitudo" to us, but precisely on that account we cannot become "beati possidentes" in the common usage of the word.

And beyond this goal lies only a last stage. The way thereto leads through death. Our evolution lies in God's hand. The eternal love which our faith experiences guarantees us blessedness in this last stage too.

What hinders the blessedness of the Christian on earth? There is a twofold hindrance, sin in him and sin around him. Blessedness becomes completely his when the sin in his heart and in the relationships of life is no more.

Such a condition we look forward to after death, in the life beyond. We believe it because we believe in God as the all-operative love. As to what changes this world will experience before that condition of perfection —who can imagine what like it will be in Berlin 500 or 1000 years after this? As to what destinies will pass over our soul in the darkness of the state of death we can only make suppositions in accordance with our faith and our world-philosophy. But we will not leave the firm ground of the religious life.

After death a new life, as we know, is to become ours. So far as our knowledge of mankind goes, we know no real state of life or relation to other living beings except in the forms of some kind of sensuous life. We can think of one whose body is mouldering as indeed existing, but not as actively alive. The soul of the dead may be conceived of after the analogy of such human conditions as those in which the soul is active without sense activity, for example, in the condition of dreams. Life with all the pleasure and power expressed in the word is somehow mediated through and conditioned by the senses. The old Christian conception of the "resurrection of the body" corresponds in its own way to what the newer psychology teaches us. Thereby it has really become a modern conception again.

And what can it be with this last stage? A falling asleep in faith in Him whose operation all is; a still dreaming of Him who is in all things; and a blessed awakening at the

THE NEW LIFE AND ITS GOAL

dawn of the day when He is all in all. Then the soul enters again in conscious activity on what was its fundamental tendency, namely, faith and love, and the golden doors of the eternal world are opened. God reigns, and we feel His glory, and are the useful, willingly serviceable organs of His sovereignty, having faith and loving, receiving and giving in accordance with our nature. This nature remains, nay, it is only then that we become completely what we are. God saves us from the world and from sin and from ourselves, and it is only thereby that we become ourselves. We are redeemed through Christ to eternal blessedness.

That is eternal blessedness. But the gay-coloured curtain of this varied world hangs before the last act of its history, and only seldom does the eye catch a glimpse of the glory behind, when the curtain is lifted by a breeze of the Spirit. But there is finally only one thing to which the heart can cling, namely, faith in the eternal Love. " Father,

I will that they also, whom Thou hast given Me, be with Me where I am"; and again, "Eye hath not seen, nor ear heard, neither have entered into the heart of man, the things which God hath prepared for them that love Him." Fancy may complete the picture— one has but to think of Dante, or of books of all kinds, whether about heaven or hell— and that is its prerogative. Let me be silent, for I think that for this too what the poet says holds good, one must not "magna parvis tenuare modis," or wed a slight melody to a great text.

Religion does not solve the last enigmas as to particular and small things, but it banishes fear of the particulars. But one thing is certain, that only those can see that world who have belonged to it here. It follows from the fact that we are what we are. No one attains to blessedness who has not attained to it in this life in faith and love. Of eternal value and an eternal organ in God's Kingdom only he can be who has been of worth and

THE NEW LIFE AND ITS GOAL 331

has become an organ of God here. It cannot be otherwise. We do not reckon with "metamorphoses"; and though we did, it is quite clear that no metamorphoses could bring blessedness as we understand it. The time of this life is short, but yet it is long enough as a way to eternal life.

This brings us to the end of our course. I hope we have not worked in vain. The sovereignty of God and faith, the Kingdom of God and love—that is the Christian religion. It brings us peace and active energy, and thereby satisfies the need of our soul. That is all. May it become something to you also. It cannot become anything to anyone without becoming his all.

www.ingramcontent.com/pod-product-compliance
Lightning Source LLC
Chambersburg PA
CBHW050836230426
43667CB00012B/2022